ISBN 0-8373-5828-0
128   ADMISSION TEST SERIES

 **RUDMAN'S QUESTIONS AND ANSWERS ON THE...**

MFT

Marital & Family Therapy Examination

Intensive preparation for the examination including...

- Thinking about Practice
- Incorporating Awareness of the Larger System
- Addressing Interpersonal and Family Process
- Attending to Therapeutic Relationships
- Assessing & Diagnosing
- Designing & Conducting Treatment
- Evaluating Ongoing Process, Outcomes, & Termination
- Maintaining Professional Ethics & Standards of Practice

NATIONAL LEARNING CORPORATION

PASSBOOK SERIES®

THE *PASSBOOK SERIES®* has been created to prepare applicants and candidates for the ultimate academic battlefield – the examination room.

At some time in our lives, each and every one of us may be required to take an examination – for validation, matriculation, admission, qualification, registration, certification, or licensure.

Based on the assumption that every applicant or candidate has met the basic formal educational standards, has taken the required number of courses, and read the necessary texts, the *PASSBOOK SERIES®* furnishes the one special preparation which may assure passing with confidence, instead of failing with insecurity. Examination questions – together with answers – are furnished as the basic vehicle for study so that the mysteries of the examination and its compounding difficulties may be eliminated or diminished by a sure method.

This book is meant to help you pass your examination provided that you qualify and are serious in your objective.

The entire field is reviewed through the huge store of content information which is succinctly presented through a provocative and challenging approach – the question-and-answer method.

A climate of success is established by furnishing the correct answers at the end of each test.

You soon learn to recognize types of questions, forms of questions, and patterns of questioning. You may even begin to anticipate expected outcomes.

You perceive that many questions are repeated or adapted so that you can gain acute insights, which may enable you to score many sure points.

You learn how to confront new questions, or types of questions, and to attack them confidently and work out the correct answers.

You note objectives and emphases, and recognize pitfalls and dangers, so that you may make positive educational adjustments.

Moreover, you are kept fully informed in relation to new concepts, methods, practices, and directions in the field.

You discover that you are actually taking the examination all the time: you are preparing for the examination by "taking" an examination, not by reading extraneous and/or supererogatory textbooks.

In short, this PASSBOOK®, used directedly, should be an important factor in helping you to pass your test.

EXAMINATION IN
MARITAL AND FAMILY THERAPY

THE PURPOSE OF THE EXAMINATION

The Association of Marital and Family Therapy Regulatory Board's (AMFTRB) Examination in Marital and Family Therapy is provided to assist state boards of examiners in evaluating the knowledge of applicants for licensure or certification. There is a wide diversity of educational backgrounds among the applicants who seek licensure or certification in marital and family therapy. AMFTRB offers a standardized examination, for use by its member boards, in order to determine if these applicants have attained the knowledge considered essential for entry-level professional practice, and in order to provide a common element in the evaluation of candidates from one state to another.

The resources of individual marital and family therapists, the AMFTRB, and the Professional Examination Service (PES) are used in the development and continuing improvement of the examination. These combined resources are greater than those available to any individual state board.

The Examination in Marital and Family Therapy is only part of the overall evaluation used by the member boards. The AMFTRB expects that candidates will be allowed to sit for the examination only after their credentials have been examined and found to meet the education and experience requirements for licensure or certification in their respective states. Such candidates are expected to have attained a broad basic knowledge of marital and family therapy, regardless of their individual backgrounds. The examination is designed to assess this knowledge through questions focused on the tasks that an entry-level marital and family therapist should be able to perform, and the knowledge required to perform those tasks successfully.

Applicants who have completed the required academic and experiential preparation and who have developed the level of competence necessary for entry-level professional practice in marital and family therapy should be able to pass the test. Neither AMFTRB, PES, nor the member boards can send copies of past examinations to applicants, nor is there a list of recommended books or other materials for use in preparation for the examination. However, the practice domains, task statements, and knowledge statements upon which the examination is based have been included in this brochure and may be helpful to candidates preparing for the examination.

TEST CONTENT AND ADMINISTRATION

The examination consists of objective multiple-choice questions covering knowledge essential to the professional practice of marital and family therapy. Each form of the examination contains 200 items and is constructed according to the test specifications. Each item has four alternative answers, only one of which is correct. Candidates are allowed four hours to complete the examination.

The reported score equals the total number of correct responses: there is no additional penalty for incorrect answers. It is to the candidate's advantage to answer each item even when uncertain of the correct response. The candidate should choose the single best answer to each item. No credit is given for items in which more than one response is selected. Sample items similar to those found on the examination are included at the end of this brochure.

The examination is administered through Prometric Thomson Learning™ centers and scored by PES, which reports the scores and relevant normative data to the administering boards. Each board sets the standard for passing in its respective state and reports the results to the candidates. All procedures and decisions with regard to licensure are the responsibility of the individual boards. Any questions about these procedures should be directed to the appropriate state board.

The Marital and Family Therapy Examination is being offered via computer. This allows candidates to test during three windows of time each year. In addition to extra exam dates candidates are able to test at a number of Prometric Thomson Learning™ centers. All candidates taking the Marital and Family Therapy examination will receive instructions concerning fees, deadlines and applications from their participating state board.

TEST SPECIFICATIONS
FOR THE EXAMINATION IN MARTIAL AND FAMILY THERAPY

PRACTICE DOMAINS

Domain 01   The Practice of Marital and Family Therapy (22.5%)
This domain encompasses tasks related to incorporating systemic theory and perspectives into practice activities, and establishing and maintaining ongoing therapeutic relationships with the client* system.

Domain 02   Assessing, Hypothesizing, and Diagnosing (22.5%)
This domain encompasses tasks related to assessing the various dimensions of the client system, forming and reformulating hypotheses, and diagnosing the client system in order to guide therapeutic activities.

Domain 03   Designing and Conducting Treatment (32.5%)
This domain encompasses tasks related to developing and implementing interventions with the client system.

Domain 04   Evaluating Ongoing Process and Terminating Treatment (7.5%)
This domain encompasses tasks related to continuously evaluating the therapeutic process and incorporating feedback into the course of treatment, as well as planning for termination.

Domain 05   Maintaining Ethical, Legal, and Professional Standards (15%)

This domain encompasses tasks related to ongoing adherence to legal and ethical codes and treatment agreements, maintaining competency in the field, and professionalism.

* The term client refers to the individual, couple, family, group, and other collaborative systems that are a part of treatment.

TASK STATEMENTS

01 The Practice of Marital and Family Therapy

01.01   Practice therapy in a manner consistent with the philosophical perspectives of the discipline.

01.02   Maintain consistency between systemic theory and clinical practice.

01.03   Integrate individual treatment approaches within systemic treatment approaches.

01.04   Demonstrate sensitivity to the client's context(s) (e.g., spirituality, gender, sexuality, culture, class, and socio-economic condition).

01.05   Establish an atmosphere of acceptance and safety by attending to the physical environment, language, and client's needs.

01.06   Establish therapeutic relationship(s) with the client system.

01.07   Attend to the interactional process between the therapist and client (e.g., therapeutic conversation, transference, and counter-transference) throughout the therapeutic process.

02 Assessing, Hypothesizing, and Diagnosing

02.01   Assess client's verbal and non-verbal communication to develop hypotheses about relationship patterns.

02.02   Identify boundaries, roles, rules, alliances, coalitions, and hierarchies by observing interactional patterns within the system.

02.03   Assess system dynamics/processes.

02.04   Assess how individual members of the client system understand their relational issues.

02.05   Formulate and continually assess hypotheses regarding the client that reflect contextual understanding.

02.06   Review background, history, context, client beliefs, external influences, and current events surrounding the origins and maintenance of the presenting issue(s).

02.07   Identify client's attempts to resolve the presenting issue(s) and the individuals in the family, community, and professional systems involved in the problem resolution process.

02.08   Assess client's level of economic, social, emotional, and mental functioning.

02.09   Assess the family life cycle stage of the client.

02.10   Assess the relationship between the individual developmental stage and the family life cycle stage.

02.11   Assess developmental stage of members of the client system for impact on problem formation, maintenance, and resolution.

02.12   Assess strengths and resources available to client.

02.13   Assess level of mental or physical risk or danger to the client (e.g., suicide, domestic violence, elder abuse).

02.14   Administer and review data from standardized and/or non-standardized tests.

02.15   Assess and diagnose client in accordance with formal diagnostic criteria (e.g.,

DSM and ICD) while maintaining a systems perspective.

02.16   Integrate diagnostic impressions with system(s) perspective/assessment when formulating treatment hypotheses.

02.17   Assess influence of individual diagnosis on the client system.

02.18   Assess influence of biological factors and medical conditions on the client system.

02.19   Identify external factors (events, transitions, illness, trauma, etc.) affecting client functioning.

02.20   Determine need for evaluation by other professional systems.

02.21   Collaborate with client, professional, and community systems, as appropriate, in establishing treatment priorities.

03 Designing and Conducting Treatment

03.01   Create therapeutic contracts.

03.02   Define short and long-term goals by organizing and interpreting assessment information, in collaboration with client as appropriate.

03.03   Develop a treatment plan reflecting a contextual understanding of presenting issues.

03.04   Develop and monitor safety plan to address identified risk (domestic violence, suicide, elder abuse).

03.05   Develop consensus on the definition of presenting issues.

03.06   Choose interventions based on application of theory and research (individual, couple, group, and family).

03.07   Construct rationale for selecting a therapeutic intervention.

03.08   Determine sequence of treatment processes and identify which members of the client system will be involved in specific tasks and stages.

03.09   Choose therapeutic modalities and interventions while considering the uniqueness of each client.

03.10   Integrate multiple types and sources of information while conducting therapy.

03.11   Collaborate with collateral systems, as appropriate, throughout the treatment process.

03.12   Use genograms and/or family mapping as therapeutic interventions when appropriate.

03.13   Facilitate change through restructure and reorganization of the client system.

03.14   Identify and explore competing priorities for client issues to be addressed in treatment.

03.15   Assist client(s) in developing decision-making and problem-solving skills.

03.16   Assist client(s) in developing appropriate verbal and non-verbal emotional communication in their relational context(s).

03.17   Attend to the homeostatic process and its impact on the system's ability to reach therapeutic goals.

03.18   Assist client to change perspective of the presenting issues to facilitate appropriate solution(s).

03.19   Influence behavior and/or perceptions through use of techniques such as metaphor, re-framing, inventiveness, creativity, humor, and prescribing the symptom.

03.20   Enable client to attempt new/alternate ways of resolving problems.

03.21   During treatment planning, identify criteria upon which to terminate treatment.

04 Evaluating Ongoing Process and Terminating Treatment

04.01 Use relevant theory and/or research data in the ongoing evaluation of process, outcomes, and termination.

04.02 Evaluate progress of therapy in collaboration with client and collateral systems as appropriate.

04.03 Modify treatment plan with client and collateral systems as appropriate.

04.04 Collaboratively plan for termination of treatment.

04.05 Terminate therapeutic relationship as appropriate.

05 Maintaining Ethical, Legal and Professional Standards

05.01 Adhere to ethical codes of relevant professional organizations and associations.

05.02 Adhere to relevant statutes, case law, and regulations affecting professional practice.

05.03 Practice in accordance with one's own area of expertise (i.e., education, training, and experience.

05.04 Maintain awareness of the influence of the therapist's own issues (e.g., family-of-origin, gender, culture, personal prejudice, value system, life experience, supervisor, etc.).

05.05 Maintain continuing competencies essential to the field (e.g., continuing education, critical reading of professional literature, attendance at workshops and professional meetings, supervision, and consultation).

05.06 Demonstrate professional responsibility and competence in forensic and legal issues (e.g., court-ordered cases, testimony, expert witness, custody hearings, etc).

05.07 Adhere to treatment agreements with clients. Respect the rights and responsibilities of clients.

05.09 Assist clients in making informed decisions relevant to treatment (e.g., filing third-party insurance claims, collateral systems, alternative treatments, limits of confidentiality).

05.10 Consult with colleagues and other professionals as necessary regarding clinical, ethical, and legal issues and concerns.

05.11 Respect the roles and responsibilities of other professionals working with the client.

05.12 Maintain accurate, timely, and thorough record keeping.

05.13 Integrate technology (e.g., Internet, fax, telephone, email) into the treatment process, as appropriate.

KNOWLEDGE STATEMENTS

01 Foundations of marital therapy and family therapy (e.g., Sullivan, Jackson, Ackerman, Bowen, Bateson, Weakland, Haley, Satir)

02 History of the marital and family therapy field

03 Family studies and science (e.g., step families, remarriage, blended families)

04 Marital studies and science

05 General Systems Theory

06 Models of family therapy and their clinical application

07 Individually based theory and therapy models (e.g., person-centered, Gestalt, RET, behavioral)

08 Impact of couple dynamics on the system

09 Family belief systems and their impact on problem formation and treatment

10 Family homeostasis as it relates to problem formation and maintenance

11   Family life cycle stages and their impact on problem formation and treatment
12   Human development throughout the lifespan (e.g., physical, emotional, social, psychological, spiritual, cognitive)
13   Human sexual anatomy, physiology, and development
14   Sexually transmitted diseases
15   Theories of personality
16   Child, adolescent, and adult psychopathology
17   Impact of developmental disorders (e.g., child and adolescent, geriatrics) on system dynamics
18   Trauma (e.g., historical, current, and anticipatory trauma)
19   Risk factors for and patterns of abuse, (abandonment, physical, emotional, verbal, sexual)
20   Risk factors, stages, and patterns of grief response for loss (death, sudden unemployment, runaway children)
21   Risk factors and relational patterns of endangerment (rape, domestic violence, suicide, self-injurious behavior)
22   Behaviors, psychological features, or physical symptoms that indicate a need for medical, educational, psychiatric, or psychological evaluation
23   Diagnostic interviewing techniques
24   Diagnostic and Statistical Manual of Mental Disorders (DSM) and International Statistical Classification of Diseases & Related Health Problems (ICD)
25   Standardized psychological assessment tests (e.g., MMPI)
26   Non-standardized assessment tests (e.g., genograms, family maps, scaling questions)
27   Relational diagnostic tests (e.g., Dyadic Adjustment Scale, Marital Satisfaction Inventory, FACES, Prepare/Enrich, etc.)
28   Dynamics of and strategies for managing transference and counter-transference (use of self of therapist, handling/control of the process of therapy)
29   Reference materials regarding medication side effects and classification
30   Effects of non-prescription substances (e.g., over the counter medications, herbals) on the client system
31   Pre-marital education and treatment
32   Divorce
33   Child custody
34   Infertility
35   Adoption
36   Infidelity
37   Trauma intervention models
38   Crisis intervention models
39   Sex therapy
40   Sexual abuse treatment for victims, perpetrators, and their families
41   Sexual behaviors and disorders associated with Internet and other forms of technology (e.g., Internet and cybersex)
42   Effect of substance abuse & dependence on individual and family functioning
43   Effects of addictive behaviors (e.g., gambling, shopping, sexual) on individual and family system
44   Addiction treatment modalities (e.g., 12-step programs, individual, couple, marital and family therapy)
45   Spiritual and religious beliefs (e.g., eastern and western philosophies) and the impact on the system in treatment
46   Impact of loss and grief on the client (e.g., death, chronic illness, economic

change, roles, and sexual potency)

47   Research literature and research methodology (including quantitative and qualitative methods) sufficient to critically evaluate assessment tools and therapy models

48   Methodologies for developing and evaluating programs (e.g., parenting, grief workshops)

49   Statutes, case law and regulations (e.g., clinical records, informed consent, confidentiality and privileged communication, privacy, fee disclosure, mandatory reporting, professional boundaries, mandated clients)

50   Codes of ethics

51   Business practices (e.g., storage and disposal of records, training of office staff, work setting policies, collections, referrals, advertising, and marketing, management of the process of therapy)

52   Use of technology (e.g., cell phones, fax machines, electronic filing of claims, Internet therapy)

53   Diversity studies (e.g., race, ethnicity, class, gender, gay & lesbian issues)

54   Neuropsychology

55   Community systems (schools, human service agencies)

56   Group mandated (e.g., anger management, domestic violence treatment, sexual offender programs) or voluntary (divorce recovery, parenting) treatment programs

MODELS OF COUPLE AND FAMILY THERAPY

Adlerian family therapy
Attachment theory
Bowen family systems theory
Cognitive behavioral therapy (e.g., Gottman, Ellis)
Collaborative language (e.g., Dan Wile)
Communication theory (e.g., Jackson, Watzlawick, Bateson)
Contextual therapy
Couple, marital, and family enrichment models
Emotionally focused therapy (e.g., Susan Johnson, Les Greenberg)
Ericksonian therapy
Experiential approaches (e.g., Satir, Whitaker)
Feminist family therapy
Medical family therapy
Milan systemic family therapy
MRI Brief therapy
Narrative therapy (e.g. ., White, Epston, Anderson)
Object relations therapy
Psychoanalytic family therapy (e.g., Ackerman)
Second order cybernetics
Solution focused therapy (e.g., DeShazer, O'Hanlon, Weiner-Davis)
Strategic therapy (e.g., Haley, Madanes)
Structural therapy (e.g., Minuchin)
Models of couple and family therapy include, but are not limited to, the listed models.

SAMPLE QUESTIONS

A. According to Minuchin, the therapist's methods for creating a therapeutic system with a family and of positioning himself/herself as its leader are known as:

1. introjection.
2. restructuring.
3. joining.
4. enacting.

B. QUESTIONS 1 AND 2 REFER TO THE FOLLOWING INFORMATION:

Mr. and Mrs. Walter have been married for 1.5 years and have a newborn baby.
They seek therapy to deal with behavioral problems involving Mrs. Walter's
three children from a previous marriage. Mr. Walter angrily says that the children, ages 9, 12 and 16, "mouth back" at him and do not respect their mother's authority. Mr. and Mrs. Walter have started having serious fights.

1. Which one of the following statements should the therapist make to help the family perceive their complaints from a systems perspective?

   1. "The children are having difficulty adapting to the new baby."
   2. "It is difficult to be a stepfather."
   3. "The marital relationship is being affected by Mrs. Walter's children."
   4. "You are experiencing a normal adjustment to becoming a stepfamily."

2. The family therapist decides to focus initially on the times when Mr. Walters has thought that the children were respecting their mother's authority. The purpose of this focus is to help the:

   1. mother perceive her part in the interaction.
   2. father accept his role as a stepparent.
   3. parents to feel hopeful about the situation and to mobilize their resources.
   4. parents unite the marital dyad.

C. A therapist working with a couple gives the following instructions:
Get ready for bed; then I want you [the wife] to lie on your belly; then you [the husband] caress her back as gently and sensitively as you can; move your hands very slowly; do no more. In the meantime, I want you [the wife] to be "selfish" and just concentrate.

The therapist is here using a technique developed by Masters and Johnson and known as:

1. guided fantasy.
2. inverse massage.
3. sexual paradox.
4. sensate focus.

D. A family is referred for therapy to a family therapist in private practice. The son, age 17, has recently been discharged from a psychiatric hospital but has remained in individual therapy with a psychiatrist. He has a history of alcoholism and since his discharge has two charges pending against him for driving while intoxicated. The parents convey to the family therapist their concern that the psychiatrist is unaware of their son's recent alcohol abuse or of the pending charges. In this situation, the most appropriate initial approach for the family therapist would be to:

1. continue to work with the family and advise the parents to call the psychiatrist so that he/she can brief the parents on their son's therapy.
2. call the psychiatrist and inform him/her of the family's turmoil and the son's drinking episodes.
3. encourage the son to talk to his therapist and ask the family members to sign a release of information form to facilitate coordination of treatment.
4. refer the son to Alcoholics Anonymous meetings and work exclusively with the parents.

E. According to Haley, a correct statement regarding system maintenance is that it:

1. is a therapeutic intervention.
2. is a therapeutic process supporting the relationship.
3. describes the therapist's non-directive effort to provide symmetrical balance.
4. may involve hidden payoffs for the resistant family.

F. In the use of videotape in working with families, the most essential condition is that:

1. the equipment remains inconspicuous.
2. all those to be taped agree to its use.
3. its use will be necessary to achieve a certain goal.
4. the worker will be personally comfortable with being taped.

ANSWERS: A. 3; B1. 4, B2. 3; C. 4; D. 3; E. 4; F. 2.

HOW TO TAKE A TEST

You have studied long, hard and conscientiously.

With your official admission card in hand, and your heart pounding, you have been admitted to the examination room.

You note that there are several hundred other applicants in the examination room waiting to take the same test.

They all appear to be equally well prepared.

You know that nothing but your best effort will suffice. The "moment of truth" is at hand: you now have to demonstrate objectively, in writing, your knowledge of content and your understanding of subject matter.

You are fighting the most important battle of your life—to pass and/or score high on an examination which will determine your career and provide the economic basis for your livelihood.

What extra, special things should you know and should you do in taking the examination?

BEFORE THE TEST

YOUR PHYSICAL CONDITION IS IMPORTANT

     If you are not well, you can't do your best work on tests. If you are half asleep, you can't do your best either. Here are some tips:

1) Get about the same amount of sleep you usually get. Don't stay up all night before the test, either partying or worrying—DON'T DO IT!
2) If you wear glasses, be sure to wear them when you go to take the test. This goes for hearing aids, too.
3) If you have any physical problems that may keep you from doing your best, be sure to tell the person giving the test. If you are sick or in poor health, you really cannot do your best on any test. You can always come back and take the test some other time.

AT THE TEST

EXAMINATION TECHNIQUES

1) Read the general instructions carefully. These are usually printed on the first page of the exam booklet. As a rule, these instructions refer to the timing of the examination; the fact that you should not start work until the signal and must stop work at a signal, etc. If there are any *special* instructions, such as a choice of questions to be answered, make sure that you note this instruction carefully.

2) When you are ready to start work on the examination, that is as soon as the signal has been given, read the instructions to each question booklet, underline any key words or phrases, such as *least, best, outline, describe* and the like. In this way you will tend to answer as requested rather than discover on reviewing your paper that you *listed without describing*, that you selected the *worst* choice rather than the *best* choice, etc.

3) If the examination is of the objective or multiple-choice type – that is, each question will also give a series of possible answers: A, B, C or D, and you are called upon to select the best answer and write the letter next to that answer on your answer paper – it is advisable to start answering each question in turn. There may be anywhere from 50 to 100 such questions in the three or four hours allotted and you can see how much time would be taken if you read through all the questions before beginning to answer any. Furthermore, if you come across a question or group of questions which you know would be difficult to answer, it would undoubtedly affect your handling of all the other questions.

4) If the examination is of the essay type and contains but a few questions, it is a moot point as to whether you should read all the questions before starting to answer any one. Of course, if you are given a choice – say five out of seven and the like – then it is essential to read all the questions so you can eliminate the two which are most difficult. If, however, you are asked to answer all the questions, there may be danger in trying to answer the easiest one first because you may find that you will spend too much time on it. The best technique is to answer the first question, then proceed to the second, etc.

5) Time your answers. Before the exam begins, write down the time it started, then add the time allowed for the examination and write down the time it must be completed, then divide the time available somewhat as follows:
   - If 3-1/2 hours are allowed, that would be 210 minutes. If you have 80 objective-type questions, that would be an average of 2-1/2 minutes per question. Allow yourself no more than 2 minutes per question, or a total of 160 minutes, which will permit about 50 minutes to review.
   - If for the time allotment of 210 minutes there are 7 essay questions to answer, that would average about 30 minutes a question. Give yourself only 25 minutes per question so that you have about 35 minutes to review.

6) The most important instruction is to *read each question* and make sure you know what is wanted. The second most important instruction is to *time yourself properly* so that you answer every question. The third most important instruction is to *answer every question*. Guess if you have to but include something for each question. Remember that you will receive no credit for a blank and will probably receive some credit if you write something in answer to an essay question. If you guess a letter – say "B" for a multiple-choice question – you may have guessed right. If you leave a blank as an answer to a multiple-choice question, the examiners may respect your

feelings but it will not add a point to your score. Some exams may penalize you for wrong answers, so in such cases *only*, you may not want to guess unless you have some basis for your answer.

7) Suggestions
   a. Objective-type questions
      1. Examine the question booklet for proper sequence of pages and questions
      2. Read all instructions carefully
      3. Skip any question which seems too difficult; return to it after all other questions have been answered
      4. Apportion your time properly; do not spend too much time on any single question or group of questions
      5. Note and underline key words – *all, most, fewest, least, best, worst, same, opposite,* etc.
      6. Pay particular attention to negatives
      7. Note unusual option, e.g., unduly long, short, complex, different or similar in content to the body of the question
      8. Observe the use of "hedging" words – *probably, may, most likely,* etc.
      9. Make sure that your answer is put next to the same number as the question
      10. Do not second-guess unless you have good reason to believe the second answer is definitely more correct
      11. Cross out original answer if you decide another answer is more accurate; do not erase until you are ready to hand your paper in
      12. Answer all questions; guess unless instructed otherwise
      13. Leave time for review

   b. Essay questions
      1. Read each question carefully
      2. Determine exactly what is wanted. Underline key words or phrases.
      3. Decide on outline or paragraph answer
      4. Include many different points and elements unless asked to develop any one or two points or elements
      5. Show impartiality by giving pros and cons unless directed to select one side only
      6. Make and write down any assumptions you find necessary to answer the questions
      7. Watch your English, grammar, punctuation and choice of words
      8. Time your answers; don't crowd material

8) Answering the essay question

Most essay questions can be answered by framing the specific response around several key words or ideas. Here are a few such key words or ideas:

M's: manpower, materials, methods, money, management
P's: purpose, program, policy, plan, procedure, practice, problems, pitfalls, personnel, public relations

a. Six basic steps in handling problems:
   1. Preliminary plan and background development
   2. Collect information, data and facts
   3. Analyze and interpret information, data and facts
   4. Analyze and develop solutions as well as make recommendations
   5. Prepare report and sell recommendations
   6. Install recommendations and follow up effectiveness

b. Pitfalls to avoid
   1. *Taking things for granted* – A statement of the situation does not necessarily imply that each of the elements is necessarily true; for example, a complaint may be invalid and biased so that all that can be taken for granted is that a complaint has been registered
   2. *Considering only one side of a situation* – Wherever possible, indicate several alternatives and then point out the reasons you selected the best one
   3. *Failing to indicate follow up* – Whenever your answer indicates action on your part, make certain that you will take proper follow-up action to see how successful your recommendations, procedures or actions turn out to be
   4. *Taking too long in answering any single question* – Remember to time your answers properly

EXAMINATION SECTION

EXAMINATION SECTION
TEST 1

Directions: Each question or incomplete statement is followed by several suggested answers or completions. Select the one the BEST answers the question or completes the statement. *PRINT THE LETTER OF THE CORRECT ANSWER IN THE SPACE AT THE RIGHT.*

1) The ultimate goal of structural family therapy can be said to be   1. _____

   A.   removing the symptom
   B.   helping clients achieve a high degree of self-differentiation
   C.   altering impediments to effective parenting
   D.   expanding the experience of emotions

2) For the therapist, assessing professional balances is probably most 2. _____
difficult in terms of

   A.   the intensity and depth of questioning
   B.   managing the timing of interventions
   C.   the room setting
   D.   the questioning of clients

3) The idea that one behavior is a stimulus, the other a response, is an 3. _____
example of

   A.   the Premack principle
   B.   prescribing the symptom
   C.   linear causality
   D.   object relations

4) In the MRI (Mental Research Institute) model of family therapy,   4. _____
the focus of treatment is on

   A.   distress
   B.   rules
   C.   systems
   D.   behavior

5) In the field of marital and family therapy, feminism has generally   5. _____
produced each of the following, except

   A.   increased awareness of cultural biases
   B.   an appreciation for the costs of privilege
   C.   specific techniques for challenging the status quo
   D.   awareness of the idea that the personal is political

6) In general, the least appropriate role for a therapist to adopt in a conjoint treatment program is that of a

6. _____

A. confronter
B. friend
C. parent
D. referee

7) Which of the following terms is used to denote the psychological separation of intellect and emotions, or the independence of self from others?

7. _____

A. Cleavage
B. Schism
C. Cutoff
D. Differentiation

8) The evaluation phase of couples therapy usually requires _____ meetings.

8. _____

A. 1 to 2
B. 2 to 4
C. 4 to 6
D. 6 to 8

9) Each of the following approaches is a type of strategic family therapy, except

9. _____

A. solution-focused therapy
B. narrative approaches
C. experiential approaches
D. communication approaches

10) From the therapist's perspective, which of the following "disguises" for anger is typically easiest to detect?

10. _____

A. Self-victimization
B. The tactic of reason and rationality
C. The adoption of righteousness
D. Passive-aggressive behavior

11) The term "affect" is often used in therapy as a substitute for the term

11. _____

A. outcome
B. mood
C. method
D. behavior

12) Object relations therapists propose that

A. an infant's contact with early caregivers exerts a profound life-long   12. _____
influence
B. symptomatic behaviors are nearly always produced by the desire for love
C. emotionally expressive households can be detrimental to a schizophrenic patient
D. relationship distress is usually a product of poor social skills

13) Which of the following best describes the purpose for a therapist's   13. _____ D
use of images and analogies for clients?

A. Forcing a confrontation with the presenting problem.
B. Deflecting attention away from a particularly painful fact of a relationship.
C. Emphasizing cognition over affect.
D. Raising the intensity and understanding of the clients' difficulties.

14) Which of the following terms is used to describe relationships   14. _____ C
based on differences which fit together, where qualities of one make up for lacks in the
other?

A. Dyadic model
B. Fusion
C. Complementary
D. Conjoint

15) Which of the following marital assessment instruments   15. _____ A
uses true/false responses divided into overlapping domains?

A. Marital Satisfaction Inventory (MSI)
B. Dyadic Adjustment Scale (DAS)
C. Marital Interaction Coding System (MICS)
D. Primary Communications Inventory (PCI)

16) The psychoeducational model of family therapy assumes that   16. _____ C
genetic predisposition determines a person's risk for illnesses such as
schizophrenia, but the disease's onset and progress is influenced by
environmental factors. This belief is known as the _____ model.

A. nature-nurture
B. object setting
C. diathesis-stress
D. benign indifference

17) During a marital therapy session, a therapist interrupts an argument   17. _____ D
between a couple with the question, "Is this what goes on at home?" This is
an example of managing intensity through

A. stronger confrontation
B. changing the structure of the discussion
C. emotional intervention
D. process questions

18) Which of the following models of family therapy is classified as historical?   C 18. _____

A. MRI
B. Experiential
C. Object relations
D. Psychoeducational

19) Marriages are sometimes classified according to their level of intimacy. In this typology, a marriage involving covert or passive-aggressive expressions of dissatisfaction would be typed as   B 19. _____

A. passive-congenial
B. devitalized
C. total
D. conflict-habituated

20) Which model of family therapy is most likely to refer to the symptomatic family member as the "stabilizing agent"?   B 20. _____

A. Strategic
B. Structural
C. Symbolic-experiential
D. Milan (systemic)

21) Each of the following statements about schizophrenia is true, except   C 21. _____

A. Families with lower levels of expressed emotions tend to provide a better environment for patients.
B. For recently released patients, insight-based models are harmful.
C. It can be caused by disturbed family communication.
D. Improved outcomes can be achieved with psychoeducational approaches.

22) During an evaluative session with a husband and wife, the couple is struggling to give the therapist an accurate and unbiased statement of their presenting problem. After listening, which of the following is probably the most appropriate restatement of the problem on the part of the therapist?   22. _____

A. You seem to have a problem with controlling your husband's behavior.
B. It's your perception that your wife is controlling.
C. I think you both share the blame for your wife's controlling behavior.
D. So your wife controls much of your behavior.

23) Which of the following is an assumption associated with systemic family therapy?   23. _____

A. Change occurs as a result of achieving specific behavioral changes
B. The behavior of each family member serves to maintain a homeostatic state
C. The objective of treatment is to disrupt negative behavior patterns
D. In dysfunctional families, rules governing the system are too lax.

24) A client states that when she goes home for the holidays,   24. _____
she seems to lose her sense of self and grows angrier with her family
each day. This is most likely an issue that would benefit from an examination from the
_____ perspective.

A. strategic
B. cognitive
C. Bowen
D. behavioral

25) Which of the following procedures would most likely be included   25. _____
in the short-term crisis intervention phase of a treatment program in the object relations
model?

A. Reducing symptoms through clarifying communication and listening with empathy
B. Offering interpretations and examining resistance
C. Eliciting material about early childhood memories
D. Gathering information about each family member's past

26) According to the schema of Bernal and Barker, which of the   26. _____
following types of communication is considered to be least sophisticated and mature?

A. Individual
B. Transactional
C. Objects
D. Relational

27) According to Laing, many families distort their children's   27. _____
experience by either denying or relabeling it, in a phenomenon known as

A. pretend technique
B. reframing
C. mystification
D. disassociation

28) In McMaster's model of family functioning, psychopathological   28. _____
families are likely to exhibit each of the following, except

A. inadequate family functions or unaccountability
B. poor problem solving
C. overly blunt communication
D. affective responsiveness in a very narrow range

29) The concept of triangulation is associated especially strongly   29. _____
with the _____ model of family therapy.

A. MRI
B. experiential
C. Bowen system
D. strategic

30) In the "involvement" stage of symbolic-experiential therapy, the therapist 30. _____

A. assesses the family system and subsystems
B. begins the battle for initiative
C. observes family interactions /
D. dictates the terms of therapy

31) In general, the three main categories of therapeutic intervention are 31. _____

A. positive, negative, and neutral
B. instructive, destructive, and constructive /
C. unilateral, bilateral, and multilateral
D. /behavioral, cognitive, and affective

32) A therapist is preparing a schematic genogram of a family system. 32. _____
Which of the following symbols is typically used to represent men?

A. Horizontal line
B. Square /
C. Vertical line
D. Circle

33) A general assumption in systemic marital therapy is that 33. _____

A. unresolved childhood feelings are usually separate from the intimacy and commitment of a marital relationship
B. because of the complementary nature of relationships, one spouse is typically more emotionally available than the other /
C. one spouse will generally resist the movement of the other if the couple's established patterns are challenged
D. when one spouse displays anger, the other withdraws

34) According to Satir, family members often demonstrate one of 34. _____
five universal patterns of interaction. Of these, which pattern is preferable in the therapist?

A. Computer
B. Leveller /
C. Distractor
D. Placator

35) Which of the following terms differs most in meaning from 35. _____
the others?

A. Interpretation
B. Reframing
C. Positive connotation /
D. Context marker

36) The behavioral model of family therapy identifies three methods by which a therapist can change a child's behavior. Which of the following is <u>not</u> one of these?

36. _____

A. Teaching alternative ways of responding to the problem
B. Altering the consequences of the behavior
C. Equalize the hierarchies involved
D. Reducing or varying antecedents associated with the problem

37) Which of the following statements is most often true of marriages between people in their mid-twenties?

37. _____

A. They often represent a first act of independent decision-making
B. They are often a matter of conforming to social expectations
C. They rarely produce a lasting relationship
D. They are usually love-matches

38) Family members who appear to be overinvolved or overprotective of another in the family often exhibit behavior that is described as

38. _____

A. transferent
B. equifinal
C. projective
D. enmeshed

39) An important deficit in most communication training models used by therapists with couples and families is in the area of

39. _____

A. the assumptions people hold
B. the emphasis on the sender, rather than the message
C. the emphasis on frequency rather than the quality of communication
D. the differentiation between types of communication

40) According to Whitaker, family therapy should:

40. _____

I. separate cognitive from affective responses
II. enhance independence and free choice
III. expand the experiencing of emotion
IV. improve emotional and behavioral congruence

A. I only
B. I and IV
C. II, III and IV
D. III and IV

41) Each of the following is an assumption associated with the strategic model of family therapy, <u>except</u>

41. _____

A. Functional families have clear organizational hierarchy.
B. People can change quickly, and therapy should be brief.
C. Developing insight in patients is not important to solving problems.
D. The dyad is the basic building block of any emotional interpersonal system.

42) According to Lewis, the "mid-range" family, as opposed to the 42. _____
optimal or severely disturbed family, is most likely to

A. exhibit constant effort at control
B. communicate poorly, if at all
C. have fixed boundaries
D. approach problems with a sense of timelessness

43) According to Bowen, a person who flees an unresolved emotional 43. _____
attachment is engaging in

A. extinction
B. cutoff
C. schism
D. differentiation

44) One of the most common problems in families and couples is that 44. _____
they filter their emotions through one emotional channel--most commonly,

A. false happiness
B. sadness or withdrawal
C. obstinacy
D. anger

45) Which of the following is a goal for the social stage of a strategic 45. _____
family treatment program?

A. Establishing rapport
B. Defining a problem
C. Quantifying behaviors
D. Assessing compliance

46) Which of the following is not a means by which a therapist typically 46. _____
attempts to increase the focus, intensity, and emotional depth of a session?

A. Responding to intense statements of feeling with silence
B. Rephrasing the client's statements of feeling in different language
C. Mimicking the language and meaning of client statements
D. Sharing one's own feelings in an open and natural way

47) What is the term for tasks that family members agree to complete, 47. _____
but which the therapist does not expect the family to accomplish?

A. Unchanneled tasks
B. Negative reinforcements
C. Negative cooperative tasks
D. Unprioritized tasks

48)   Which of the following steps in conflict resolution is typically   48. _____
initiated <u>first</u> by a therapist?

A.   Exploring the family of origin
B.   A lesson in fair fighting
C.   Bibliotherapy
D.   Assessing the function of conflict in the relationship

49)   According to the Bowen systems model of family therapy,   49. _____
improvements occur when

A.   the family limits its focus to the nuclear unit
B.   an emotional cutoff is reversed
C.   clients distinguish between cognitive and affective functioning
D.   the marital dyad stabilizes

50)   The Family Cohesion and Adaptability Evaluation Scale (FACES)   50. _____
is an assessment instrument that is probably best for measuring

A.   behavior control
B.   communications
C.   roles/coalitions
D.   affectivity

KEY (CORRECT ANSWERS)

1.	A	41.	D
2.	A	42.	A
3.	C	43.	B
4.	A	44.	D
5.	C	45.	A
6.	C	46.	B
7.	D	47.	C
8.	B	48.	C
9.	C	49.	D
10.	D	50.	B
11.	B		
12.	A		
13.	D		
14.	C		
15.	A		
16.	C		
17.	D		
18.	C		
19.	B		
20.	D		
21.	C		
22.	B		
23.	B		
24.	C		
25.	A		
26.	C		
27.	C		
28.	C		
29.	D		
30.	B		
31.	D		
32.	B		
33.	C		
34.	B		
35.	A		
36.	C		
37.	B		
38.	D		
39.	A		
40.	C		

TEST 2

Directions: Each question or incomplete statement is followed by several suggested answers or completions. Select the one the BEST answers the question or completes the statement. *PRINT THE LETTER OF THE CORRECT ANSWER IN THE SPACE AT THE RIGHT.*

1) Sometimes a family therapist may attempt to alter a family's hierarchy by forming an unstated alliance with one or more members. This method is known as

1. _____

A. reciprocity
B. intensity
C. upsetting
D. unbalancing

2) In an intersystem assessment for a married couple, which of the following is considered an element of the interactional system?

2. _____

A. Cognitive distortions
B. Triangles
C. Emotional contracts
D. Closeness-distance issues

3) The most significant difficulties therapists encounter in implementing the Milan approach are

3. _____

A. extensive training requirements and "one size fits all" prescriptions
B. rigidity of task assignments and dyadic limitations
C. focus on post-session change and lack of treatment standards
D. personnel splitting and shifting treatment format

4) What type of family coalition is represented in the diagram below?

4. _____

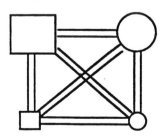

A. Functional
B. Skewed
C. Schismatic
D. Pseudodemocratic

5)   In stage one of a treatment program in the human validation   5. _____
process model, the therapist

A.   increases confusion and disorder
B.   clarifies faulty communication
C.   investigates the present problem
D.   allows for a period of emotional rest

6)   A family is in therapy, in part to explore the son's habitual truancy.   6. _____
The mother believes the son skips school specifically to get his father's
attention. This explanation can be described as

A.   dyadic
B.   triadic
C.   transferent
D.   monadic

7)   Which of the following is <u>not</u> an example of a therapist using   7. _____
inclusive language?

A.   "You are both being very hurtful to each other."
B.   "Can you understand why she feels neglected?"
C.   "Can you see how you both contribute to the problem?"
D.   "You two are similar in the way you handle stress."

8)   In general, the biggest difference between solution-focused and   8. _____
other brief models of family therapy is

A.   the use of external observation teams
B.   the framing of the problem as an enemy to the family
C.   the use of the pretend technique
D.   the time spent determining problem parameters

9)   The cognitive component of Sternberg's "triangle of love"   9. _____
model is

A.   commitment
B.   interdependence
C.   passion
D.   intimacy

10)   Which of the following models of family therapy requires   10. _____
psychoanalytic training for its practitioners?

A.   Object relations
B.   Experiential
C.   Behavioral
D.   Bowen systems

11)   During a conjoint therapy session, a woman client begins to cry.   11. _____
If the therapist is thinking in a linear manner, he/she will be led to

A.   note how the woman's spouse responds to her crying
B.   ask if her mother ever cried like that
C.   ask the client to pull herself together so the session may continue
D.   ask who or what caused her to cry

12)   In systems theory, a system tends to regulate itself in order to   12. _____
maintain a constant internal environment in response to changes in the
external environment. This tendency is known as

A.   stagnation
B.   homeostasis
C.   equipotentiality
D.   inertia

13)   In general, a therapist in a conjoint treatment program   13. _____

A.   should contain his or her interpretations until after the joining process has been
completed
B.   may offer simple interpretations during the evaluation phase that will lead the clients
toward a shared definition of the problem
C.   should not offer interpretations at all, but simply steer those of the clients
D.   should base all interpretations in history

14)   A typical Bowenian family treatment program is divided into the   14. _____
two distinct phases of

A.   session and post-session
B.   symptom remediation and intrapsychic reconstruction
C.   planning and implementation
D.   nuclear family focus and extended family focus

15)   Therapists who are AAMFT members are forbidden from   15. _____

A.   disclosing confidences under any circumstances
B.   using the AAMFT designation in public information or advertisements
C.   having sexual relations with former clients
D.   charging a client for a referral

16)   Which of the following is an open-ended question?   16. _____

A.   Have there been any more incidents?
B.   Did you do your homework last week?
C.   Have you been feeling sad?
D.   Where would you like to begin?

17)   Lidz's term for marital conflict that is pathological and overt is   17. _____

A.   marital skew
B.   asymmetry
C.   marital schism
D.   marital opposition

18) Between married couples in the 40-42 age group, marital conflict   18. _____
is most likely to have its roots in

A.   conflicting ties to the family of origin
B.   uncertainty about the choice of partner
C.   different perceptions of success
D.   rekindled fears of desertion

19) According to Madanes, helplessness is   19. _____

A.   the last resort of members at the bottom of the family hierarchy
B.   inherent rather than learned
C.   usually imagined rather than real
D.   an opportunity to manipulate social behavior

20) Each of the following is a potential benefit of the use of individual   20. _____
sessions in conjoint therapy, except

A.   the elimination of confidentiality concerns
B.   a deeper psychological or psychiatric assessment without client self-consciousness
C.   a closer tie of each partner to the therapist
D.   an enrichment of the therapist's understanding of families-of-origin

21) By far, the largest accumulation of behavior change techniques   21. _____
exists in the _____ model of family therapy.

A.   MRI
B.   behavioral
C.   functional
D.   structural

22) In communication training, which of the following is typically   22. _____
performed first?

A.   Feedback
B.   Modeling
C.   Reinforcement
D.   Rehearsal

23) During an argument about the proper time for their daughter's   23. _____
curfew, the daughter enters the room and is drawn into the argument
by the father, to side with him against the mother. This is an example of

A.   split filial loyalty
B.   triangulation
C.   diffusion
D.   enmeshment

24)   A therapist seeks to gain a thorough systemic understanding of   24. _____
a client's avowed depression. The most appropriate question for the therapist
to ask would be

A.   When did you first notice the depression?
B.   How does your spouse respond to your depression?
C.   What caused the depression?
D.   At what time did a friend or family member first comment on the depression?

25)   What is the family therapy term for a person's internalized images   25. _____
of self and others based on early parent-child interactions?

A.   Generational transmissions
B.   Object relations
C.   Invisible loyalties
D.   Acquired directives

26)   An adult client complains to the therapist that his mother often   26. _____
walks into his house unannounced, without even ringing the doorbell. This is a situation
which would probably be best handled from the _____ perspective.

A.   strategic
B.   Bowenian
C.   behavioral
D.   structural

27)   In the narrative model of family therapy, families are viewed as   27. _____

A.   single living organisms
B.   political entities with an imbalance of power
C.   victims of an oppressor
D.   systems out of balance

28)   Therapists are prone to committing several common errors when   28. _____
working with problem drinkers and their spouses. Which of the following
is not commonly one of these?

A.   Underestimating the homeostatic role drinking plays in the relationship
B.   Underestimating the degree of anger in the couple
C.   Allying with the non-alcoholic spouse against a noncompliant, alcoholic client
D.   Overestimating the clients' motivation to change

29)   The functional model of family therapy, developed by Alexander   29. _____
et al., combines elements from which of the following models?

A.   MRI and object relations
B.   General systems and behavioral
C.   Strategic and MRI
D.   Experiential and behavioral

30) Assertive language can be described as each of the following, except

30. _____

A. objective
B. differentiated
C. direct
D. free of judgement

31) The symbol below is used by structural family therapists to denote

31. _____

A. a rigid boundary
B. involvement
C. a diffuse boundary
D. overinvolvement

32) When asked to explain his tendency to lose his temper, a father says, "I can't help the way I act. My crazy family drives me to it." Of the four methods of destructive linear attribution identified by Strong and Claiborn, the father is practicing

32. _____

A. debilitation
B. justification
C. rationalization
D. vilification

33) The concept of multigenerational processes of psychopathology is closely associated with the ideas of

33. _____

A. Bowen
B. Bateson
C. White
D. Minuchin

34) Which of the following is not an advantage associated with the use of self-report questionnaires as marital assessment instruments?

34. _____

A. Ease of administration
B. Good reliability and validity
C. High degree of cognitive exposition
D. High stability over time

35) According to the MRI model of family therapy, relationships are either

35. _____

A. symmetrical or complementary
B. balanced or unbalanced
C. prescriptive or spontaneous
D. equifinal or equipotential

36) Which of the following statements or questions, spoken from one spouse to another, is probably intended to establish distance?

36. _____

A. I need a hug.
B. Would you like to spend some time together?
C. I'm really angry with you and would like to talk
D. Why did you do this to me?

37) The Milan approach attempts to induce second-order changes in families through each of the following methods, except

37. _____

A. circular questioning
B. behavior change task assignments
C. enactment
D. positive connotations

38) In severely disturbed families, separation and loss are most likely to be dealt with by

38. _____

A. an extension of one's identity beyond the family
B. recreating old parental relationships in current relationships
C. demonstrating psychotic behaviors
D. indulging in fantasy and denial

39) During a family's first session of therapy, most of the family members refer to the identified patient, a 15-year-old son, as "lazy." One of the therapist's first goals should be

39. _____

A. reframing
B. enactment
C. restraining
D. prescribing the symptom

40) The idea that individuals face a fundamental tension--attempting to satisfy opposing needs for familial connection and personal autonomy-- is one of the cornerstones of the model devised by

40. _____

A. Jackson
B. Whitaker
C. Satir
D. Bowen

41)   A married couple presents to a therapist with what they describe   41. _____
as a severe marital conflict. A good first step for the therapist to take would be to

A.   help the couple recognize that conflict exists in all close relationships
B.   help the couple to determine whether they want to remain in the relationship at all
C.   give examples of couples who have experienced or are experiencing worse conflicts
D.   ask them to explain the source of the conflict

42)   In structural family therapy, the therapist attempts to correct   42. _____
faulty family structures by

A.   focusing one-one-one with the identified patient
B.   increasing positive reinforcement of good behaviors
C.   isolating certain groups of family members to determine which combinations
produce the symptomatic behaviors
D.   altering family interaction patterns

43)   Which of the following statements is generally supported by   43. _____
research in marital communication?

A.   Nonverbal behavior is a powerful discriminator between distressed and
nondistressed couples
B.   Marital satisfaction is highly correlated to the degree with which couples stick to
one or two simple communication styles
C.   Distressed spouses do not perceive their partners' remarks as significantly less
positive than do non-distressed spouses
D.   Totally open, uncensored communication is more common in nondistressed
relationships

44)   The idea that therapists should undergo therapy as a part of their   44. _____
professional training and development is supported by each of the following
models, except

A.   MRI
B.   Human validation process
C.   Bowen systems
D.   object relations

45)   In a conjoint therapy setting, the safest interpretations for a therapist 45. _____
to make are usually

A.   general and psychoanalytical
B.   linear and unilateral
C.   individualized and historical
D.   systemic and bilateral

46)   Which of the following statements about a behavioral family   46. _____
therapy assessment is true?

A.   It occurs only during intake
B.   It focuses on the motivations for behavior
C.   It is the sole measure of determining treatment effectiveness
D.   It ignores antecedents and consequences

47) Which of the following assessment instruments is classified as "spouse-report"?

47. _____

A. Primary Communication Inventory (PCI)
B. Marital Happiness Scale (MHS)
C. Couples Interaction Scoring System (CISS)
D. Marital Satisfaction Time Line (MSTL)

48) According to Minuchin, a family with overly rigid boundaries around individuals may produce a situation of

48. _____

A. disengagement
B. regression
C. enmeshment
D. restructuring

49) In the age group of 18-22, marriage most often represents

49. _____

A. an abandonment of one's family of origin
B. an act of rebellion
C. a search for a surrogate parent
D. a major step in individuation

50) Of the following, which is most likely to be the reason a couple or family decides to terminate therapy early in the process?

50. _____

A. External events have altered the system so that the presenting problem no longer exists.
B. Problems are too painful to be faced.
C. One or more clients perceive the therapist to be unbalanced.
D. The therapist is too confrontational.

KEY (CORRECT ANSWERS)

1.	D		41.	A
2.	C		42.	D
3.	D		43.	A
4.	D		44.	A
5.	C		45.	D
6.	A		46.	C
7.	B		47.	A
8.	D		48.	A
9.	A		49.	C
10.	A		50.	C
11.	D			
12.	B			
13.	A			
14.	D			
15.	D			
16.	D			
17.	C			
18.	C			
19.	D			
20.	A			
21.	A			
22.	B			
23.	B			
24.	B			
25.	B			
26.	D			
27.	C			
28.	A			
29.	B			
30.	A			
31.	D			
32.	B			
33.	A			
34.	C			
35.	A			
36.	D			
37.	C			
38.	D			
39.	A			
40.	D			

TEST 3

Directions: Each question or incomplete statement is followed by several suggested answers or completions. Select the one the BEST answers the question or completes the statement. *PRINT THE LETTER OF THE CORRECT ANSWER IN THE SPACE AT THE RIGHT.*

1) Of the five stages involved in a strategic family treatment interview, which occurs <u>last</u>?   1. _____

A. The interaction stage
B. The task-setting stage
C. The goal-setting stage
D. The problem stage

2) A therapist wants to describe the condition of enmeshment for a couple, but wants to avoid professional jargon. She decides upon the use of an analogy. Which of the following is most suitable?   2. _____

A. Being caught in the same net.
B. Going from the frying pan to the fire.
C. Playing for opposing teams during the same game.
D. Going skydiving and using the same parachute at the same time.

3) A couple seeks a family therapist's help in dealing with their 13-year-old son, who has a history of depression. The family has recently moved and the son will enter a new school in the fall. In the first session, the family spends a great deal of time cataloguing the recent events that they believe might have contributed to the son's depression. As a follow-up to this session, a therapist using the object relations approach would probably   3. _____

A. request earlier histories in some detail
B. request that the family enact the son's first day at school
C. provide the family with some basic facts about depression
D. assure the family that many 13-year-olds experience periods of depression

4) Which of the following is <u>not</u> a frequent purpose for systemic questioning in marital or family therapy?   4. _____

A. Rooting out the causes of dysfunctional behavior
B. Making clients aware of the different levels of resistance
C. Pointing out the lack of reinforcement given to change
D. Increasing the likelihood of movement

5) Which of the following suppositions serves as the foundation of the 5. _____
MRI model of family therapy?

A. aberrant behavior reflects internal conflict
B. people's behaviors are motivated primarily by the desire for power and control over
their environments
C. individuals are reactors to information via social reaction
D. problems typically arise from unacknowledged past trauma

6) In expressive dynamic therapy, the therapist uses the context of   6. _____
_____ to employ such techniques as clarification, confrontation, and
interpretation.

A. neutrality
B. hyperactivity
C. authority
D. pseudodemocracy

7) Over a series of treatment sessions, a family therapist notes that the 7. _____
mother and father, whose conflict was the initial and primary reason for their
referral, have gradually focused their attention on the behaviors of their teenage daughter,
casting her in a generally negative light while seemingly gaining some stability in their own
relationship. The couple have exhibited an example of

A. triangulation
B. reframing
C. transference
D. projective identification

8) When treating one spouse individually for problems in the   8. _____
marriage, the use of empathy tends to involve each of the following risks, <u>except</u>

A. the alignment of the spouse and the therapist against the other
B. the inhibition of reflection
C. the viewing of the therapist as more empathetic than the client's spouse
D. the viewing of the therapist as unsympathetic to the client's spouse

9) According to the strategic model, a symptom occurs when   9. _____

A. a family system stagnates
B. a subsystem fails to conform
C. there is a power struggle in the system
D. a cross-generational coalition is formed

10) According to the behavioral model, inappropriate aggressive and   10. _____
antisocial behaviors exhibited by children

A. are symptomatic of trauma
B. begin prior to adolescence
C. have little to do with the child's parents
D. most often originate at school

11) Which of the following models of family therapy is classified as ahistorical?

11. _____

A. Object relations
B. Bowen system
C. Strategic
D. Experiential

12) In the early stages of conjoint couple therapy, a therapist should probably intervene actively and directly to keep clients from

12. _____

A. making incorrect interpretations
B. rehashing the past
C. incorrectly identifying the problem
D. blaming one another

13) The Bowenian genogram symbol below denotes

13. _____

A. The death of a female
B. The death of a male
C. The birth of a female
D. The birth of a male

14) During the first few sessions of marital therapy, a wife begins to give her husband compliments. The husband dismisses her remarks as a ploy designed to get him off her back and to satisfy the therapist. This is an example of

14. _____

A. introjection
B. cognitive distortion
C. counterdependency
D. projection

15) In a structural treatment program, which of the following would the therapist typically do first?

15. _____

A. Tracking
B. Creating objectives
C. Attending to the presenting problem
D. Assessing the family structure

16) In general, the most complex and time-consuming type of contract used in a therapeutic setting is the _____ contract.

16. _____

A. covenant
B. quid pro quo
C. noncontingent
D. good faith

17) When the "triangle" model of love is used in marital therapy, its initial use focuses on the exploration of   17. _____

A. the level of passion
B. commitment and areas of deficiency
C. fears and family-of-origin
D. the desire for intimacy

18) Which of the following is not typically a purpose involved in an intake interview?   18. _____

A. Collection of assessment information
B. Implementation of initial therapeutic regimes
C. Relation of opinions formed about relationships
D. Development of therapeutic working relationship

19) Which of the following is/are concepts associated with the MRI model of family therapy?   19. _____

    I. Equifinality
    II. Pars-pro-toto
    III. Circular causality
    IV. Quid pro quo

A. I and III
B. I, III and IV
C. II and IV
D. I, II, III and IV

20) In order to be effective, marital contracts should require a(n) _____ review of an individual's progress.   20. _____

A. hourly
B. daily
C. weekly
D. monthly

21) A family is referred to a family therapist in private practice.   21. _____
During the first few sessions a pattern is revealed in the interaction between the mother and daughter: several times in the past few months, the mother has been required to leave town for a few days, either on business or to care for her aging father. On a few of these occasions, the daughter exhibited extreme behaviors, once drinking so heavily that she ended up in a hospital emergency room, and another time ending up in the local jail after an incident of vandalism involving several other adolescents. When the mother is in town, problems such as these have never arisen. Which of the following initial impressions is most reasonable?

A. The daughter is disengaging from the mother.
B. The daughter is exhibiting pseudohostility.
C. The daughter is engaging in triangulation.
D. The daughter is practicing aversive control.

22) Ellis's rational-emotive therapy focuses on   22. _____

A.   what people think
B.   how people think
C.   what people feel
D.   how people feel

23) During a marital therapy session, the husband says flatly to his   23. _____
wife, "You're stupid." This is an example of

A.   personalization
B.   distracting
C.   polarization
D.   invalidation

24) In the initial evaluation of a family or couple, a therapist faces   24. _____
"choice points" that are both substantive and technical. Which of the
following is a substantive choice point?

A.   Whether to use individualized or standardized measurements of functioning
B.   The proper pacing of the assessment
C.   Whether to initiate the joining process or observe the family as an outsider
D.   Whether to focus on current functioning or historical background

25) Which of the following is most likely to be a reason for a couple   25. _____
to leave therapy?

A.   Therapist is perceived as too controlling
B.   Lack of interaction between therapist and clients
C.   Altered perception of the presenting problem
D.   Decision to end the marriage

26) In the clinical application of the "triangle" model of love in marital   26. _____
therapy, which of the following questions should be asked last?

A.   What prevents the identification and expression of the three components of the
triangle
B.   Whether each partner has realistic perceptions of what love involves
C.   Whether each partner has a realistic perception of what he or she can offer or has
been able to offer
D.   Whether both partners desire all three components of the triangle

27) During a conjoint session, a wife states that her husband is never   27. _____
affectionate to her. The husband responds by saying, "I am too! Just last
night I reached out to you!" The circular pattern of communication demonstrated here is

A.   Affect and cognition
B.   Thought and feeling
C.   Anger and withdrawal
D.   Attack and defend

28) As an experiential treatment technique, family sculpting is generally 28. _____
thought to produce each of the following benefits, except

A. revealing historical influences on current functioning
B. releasing unexpressed emotion
C. modeling more nurturing relationships between parent and child
D. providing more accurate information about family functioning than is available
through verbalizations

29) A family therapist who is active, directive, and central in the 29. _____
family's pattern of communication is often described as a(n)

A. joiner
B. facilitator
C. modeler
D. conductor

30) In the narrative model of family therapy, the therapist and family 30. _____
seek to achieve situations in which the problem did not occur, though the
likelihood was high that it should have occurred. Such occasions are referred to as

A. externalizations
B. unique outcomes
C. extinctions
D. second-order changes

31) Which of the following marital assessment instruments is most 31. _____
frequently used as a screening device to differentiate between satisfied and dissatisfied
couples?

A. Marital Satisfaction Inventory (MSI)
B. Marital Adjustment Scale (MAS)
C. Verbal Problem Checklist (VPC)
D. Client Satisfaction Questionnaire (CSQ)

32) In most traditional families, the wife's role is described as 32. _____

A. expressive
B. prescriptive
C. instrumental
D. projective

33) A family in which at least one child is parentified is most likely to 33. _____
produce an individual with a fear of

A. anger
B. dependency
C. responsibility
D. rejection

34) The objective of the Milan approach to family therapy is best described as   34. _____

A. activating the family's inherent capacity to generate its own solutions
B. intensifying the symptom until it is untenable
C. directing specific behavioral changes within each system
D. helping the family to change

35) A married couple, after several sessions of therapy, have developed   35. _____
an awareness that in their relationship, anger is triggered by not feeling loved.
In terms of the schema proposed by Bernal and Barker, this couple has achieved
communication at the _____ level.

A. Relational
B. Individual
C. Transactional
D. Contextual

36) During an initial session with a family, a behavioral therapist   36. _____
seeks to determine the contingencies of a child's problem behavior. Part
of the determination includes information about the characteristics of the
parents' response. The therapist will need to determine each of the following
response characteristics, except

A. frequency
B. time
C. intensity
D. duration

37) According to Satir, the main source of problems in families is   37. _____

A. a situational stressor
B. low self-esteem arising in the primary family triad
C. lax rules governing the family system
D. tension originating in the marital dyad

38) Sometimes family members adopt the façade of a harmonious   38. _____
relationship in order to avoid close relationships. This is the phenomenon known as

A. tracking
B. fusion
C. pseudomutuality
D. subtext

39) The use of analogy during treatment is described as a(n)   39. _____
_____ device for providing another view of feelings and thoughts.

A. projective
B. denotative
C. surreptitious
D. transferent

40)   The therapist assumes the role of a teacher of skills in the   40. _____
_____ model of therapy.

A.   MRI
B.   Milan
C.   strategic
D.   behavioral

41)   According to the behavioral model of family therapy, the primary   41. _____
reason for the failure of treatment of inappropriate child behavior is

A.   the therapist's failure to develop alternate contingencies
B.   child resistance
C.   martial dissatisfaction
D.   parental inconsistency

42)   A married couple presents to a therapist with what they describe   42. _____
as "communication problems." Before designing a program of treatment,
the therapist suggests that they adopt a set of assumptions to help them with
their relationship. Which of the following would least likely be included in these
recommended assumptions?

A.   The assumption of goodwill
B.   The assumption of commitment
C.   The assumption of behaviors with multiple meanings
D.   The assumption of understanding

43)   In order to observe and then change transactions which make   43. _____
up a family structure, which of the following procedures is likely to be
used by a structural family therapist?

A.   Reframing
B.   Enactment
C.   Genography
D.   Pretend technique

44)   The common methods of being passive-aggressive include   44. _____

       I.   aggrandizing
       II.   misunderstanding
       III. procrastinating
       IV.   forgetting

A.   I only
B.   II, III and IV
C.   III and IV only
D.   I, II, III and IV

45)   A client in session reports that she needs to begin exercising   45. _____
caution in discussing sensitive topics at work. The therapist responds
that it is sad when co-workers prove to be untrustworthy. This is an example of the
technique of

A.   emotional linkage
B.   countertransference
C.   derivation
D.   interpretation

46)   A man comes to a therapist by himself for counseling, saying   46. _____
his marriage is in trouble but his wife does not want to participate in therapy.
The therapist begins treating the husband individually, and requests that he
periodically press the wife to attend a conjoint session. The most likely
result of this is that the

A.   husband will lose more power in the relationship
B.   presenting problem will decrease in importance
C.   wife's position will be weakened
D.   wife will be moved to attend by her husband's clear concern

47)   Each of the following is typically recommended for schizophrenics   47. _____
and their family members, except

A.   structural family therapy
B.   promoting an attitude of benign indifference
C.   giving the family information about the onset and origin of the illness
D.   permitting family members to express frustration in the patient's presence

48)   During therapy, a mother says to her son, "You did a terrible job of 48. _____
that." Which of the following replies on the part of the son would be classified
as a "response" rather than a "reaction"?

A.   I don't really care what you think--I know I did a good job.
B.   You did an even worse job, if you ask me.
C.   I did not.
D.   What do you mean?

49)   When assigning out-of-session tasks to clients, a therapist should   49. _____
avoid

A.   making a prescription without the input of the clients
B.   approaching the prescribed behaviors systematically
C.   breaking goals down into smaller sub-goals
D.   practicing assigned behaviors in-session

50)   The foundations of the behavioral model of family therapy include   50. _____
an outline of specific procedures for improving parenting skills. Which of
the following is not one of these procedures?

A.   Learning to observe
B.   Establishing a baseline
C.   Generalizing from behaviors
D.   Negotiating a contract

KEY (CORRECT ANSWERS)

1.	B		41.	D
2.	D		42.	C
3.	A		43.	B
4.	A		44.	B
5.	C		45.	A
6.	A		46.	A
7.	A		47.	D
8.	D		48.	D
9.	C		49.	A
10.	B		50.	C
11.	C			
12.	B			
13.	A			
14.	B			
15.	A			
16.	A			
17.	B			
18.	C			
19.	D			
20.	B			
21.	D			
22.	A			
23.	A			
24.	D			
25.	B			
26.	C			
27.	D			
28.	C			
29.	D			
30.	B			
31.	B			
32.	A			
33.	A			
34.	A			
35.	A			
36.	C			
37.	B			
38.	C			
39.	A			
40.	D			

EXAMINATION SECTION
TEST 1

Directions: Each question or incomplete statement is followed by several suggested answers or completions. Select the one the BEST answers the question or completes the statement. *PRINT THE LETTER OF THE CORRECT ANSWER IN THE SPACE AT THE RIGHT.*

1) For most married couples in the 22-28 age group, the status of intimacy can usually be described as

1. _____

A. deepening but ambivalent
B. threatened by boredom
C. increasingly distant
D. fragile

2) At the system level, the MRI model of family therapy changes

2. _____

A. structures
B. rules
C. metaphors
D. behaviors

3) A couple is referred to a therapist by a colleague who has described them as very hostile and enmeshed. For the initial session, the couple should be seated

3. _____

A. together, facing the therapist
B. with their backs to each other
C. together, facing each other
D. on opposite sides of the therapist, with one on the right, one on the left

4) According to Minuchin, maladaptive transactions within a family may be changed by means of a process known overall as

4. _____

A. intensity
B. shaping
C. relabeling
D. extinction

5) Therapists usually find the need to apply the various therapeutic strategies and techniques differentially. Which of the following is not a guideline for the application of strategies?

5. _____

A. Problems involving ruminative anxiety magnifiers need treatment focused on cognitive control.
B. Problems determined by habit formation and disorders should be approached from the structural perspective.
C. Defenses that lead to impulsive, emotional activity need externally focused treatments.
D. If the problem is a "neurotic-like" disorder, therapy aimed at conflict resolution is needed.

6)   A client has several times attempted suicide. The therapist asks   6. _____
the client to explore what life would be like after his death, including who
his wife might remarry, how long his family might mourn, and how his
children might perform in school. This is an example of the experiential technique of

A.   modeling fantasy alternatives to actual stressors
B.   separating interpersonal from intrapersonal family stress
C.   affective confrontations
D.   augmenting client despair

7)   A therapist begins work with a married couple on developing an   7. _____
understanding of the "triangle" model of love. In this model, each of the
following factors is related to the idea of commitment, <u>except</u>

A.   trustworthiness
B.   an understanding of the partners' identity as a couple
C.   past rewards
D.   the attractiveness of alternative relationships

8)   Which of the following words would be used to describe   8. _____
a change in a family system that maintains stability without changing
the structure of the family or the means by which is maintains its stability?

A.   Surface
B.   Mimetic
C.   Second-order
D.   First-order

9)   A therapist and a husband and wife together develop a contract   9. _____
that includes the following agreement: Lisa want John to stop working at
5:00 exactly, so that the two can walk around Spring Lake together before
sundown. John wants Lisa to help him organize the family files for at least two hours on
the weekend. They agree that if Lisa helps out with the files for two hours, John will come
home from work by 5:00 and they will go for their walk. This is an example of a(n)
_____ contract.

A.   covenant
B.   quid pro quo
C.   conditional
D.   good faith

10)   During a session, a husband states that though he doesn't know   10. _____
why, he tends to distance himself from the people he loves most. Most
likely, this situation would be best approached from the _____ perspective.

A.   contextual
B.   object relations
C.   cognitive
D.   narrative

11) The Beavers Timberlawn Rating Scale (B-T) is an assessment device that is generally good for rating each of the following dimensions of family functioning, except

11. _____

A. affectivity
B. roles/coalitions
C. behavior control
D. problem-solving

12) A young couple with a marriage that is not yet a year old, in their first marital therapy session, describe themselves as extremely unhappy and report numerous episodes of domestic violence. The wife is in tears, and asks the therapist whether the marriage is worth saving. The therapist should

12. _____

A. recommend divorce, given the domestic violence
B. tell the couple that a divorce is their decision alone
C. advise a trial separation
D. contact the police about the domestic violence

13) In the medical model, the major strategy in reducing family resistance to therapy is

13. _____

A. psychopharmacology
B. rationale
C. rehabilitation
D. psychoeducation

14) Which of the following types of programs would generally be most detrimental to a post-release schizophrenic patient?

14. _____

A. a supervised re-entry into the home environment
B. an active foster home
C. an unsupervised re-entry into the home environment
D. a residential cooperative with autistic clients

15) Cognitive theories postulate that

15. _____

A. a person's behavior shapes his or her thinking
B. thinking is unrelated to feeling and doing
C. a person's emotions are the driving force behind his or her thinking
D. behavior and affect follow thinking

16) The term for the reinforcement of behavioral change in small steps is

16. _____

A. ascension
B. incrementalization
C. graduation
D. shaping

17)   A married couple has a chronic tendency to appear as much as   17. _____
15 minutes late for their appointed hour of therapy. Usually, when she's
able, the therapist accommodates them by exceeding the allotted hour. In this
case, the therapist

A.   is at risk for triangulation
B.   is colluding with the couple in their resistance and manipulation
C.   is behaving as professionally as is possible under the circumstances
D.   is demonstrating the kind of flexibility and care that will earn client confidence

18)   According to Rapoport, there are three intrapersonal tasks involved   18. _____
in preparing for marriage. Which of the following is not one of these?

A.   Establishing a couple identity
B.   Accommodating patterns of premarital life to patterns of the newly formed
relationship
C.   Making oneself ready to take over the role of husband or wife
D.   Disengaging, or altering the form of the engagement, from close relationships that
compete or interfere with the new marital relationship

19)   A teenage girl has a habit of coming home after curfew. As part   19. _____
of a strategic therapy program, the therapist recommends that each time she
does so, her parents require her to let them each sleep an extra thirty minutes
in the morning while she makes them breakfast and then washes the breakfast
dishes. This is an example of

A.   manipulating the symptom
B.   restraining the change
C.   a triangle
D.   an ordeal

20)   The use of marital contracting in therapy can be traced to the   20. _____
development of _____ therapy.

A.   behavioral
B.   intrapsychic
C.   cognitive
D.   systemic

21)   According to structural theory, rigid barriers within a family   21. _____
system produce subsystems that are

A.   redundant
B.   disengaged
C.   stagnant
D.   rigid

22)   Approximately what percentage of married couples who separate   22. _____
eventually get back together?

A.   30
B.   50
C.   70
D.   90

23)   Treatment of two or more persons, seen separately and usually   23. _____
by different therapists, is known as _____ therapy.

A.   concurrent
B.   dynamic
C.   conjoint
D.   symmetrical

24)   A client states that he had a "bad week." In order to create intensity   24. _____
and focus, the most appropriate response for the therapist would be to say:

A.   What made the week bad?
B.   It's not the worst week you've had, is it?
C.   Why was the week so awful?
D.   I know what you mean. My week was pretty bad too?

25)   During the work day, a private-practice therapist engages in casual   25. _____
conversation with her assistant. The assistant reveals that he and his wife have
been having problems, and indicates a desire to get counseling. Which of the following
actions would be most appropriate on the part of the therapist?

A.   Offer advice and support about the relationship while making sure the context is
casual and non-clinical
B.   As a favor to the assistant, who is a loyal and dedicated worker, offering a course
of therapy at an employee discount.
C.   Referring the assistant to a known and trusted colleague for therapy.
D.   Offering a course of therapy that will make no distinction between the assistant and
any other clients.

26)   In an integrated approach designed to enhance the intimacy of   26. _____
marital clients, the therapist reviews the identified components of intimacy
and asks the clients to discuss each one in turn. The next step in the process will be

A.   contextual
B.   structural
C.   strategic
D.   behavioral

27)   Which of the following techniques is/are associated with the   27. _____
Milan approach?

       I.   Genogram
       II.   Family triangle
       III. Invariant prescription
       IV.   Circular questioning

A.   I and II
B.   II and III
C.   III and IV
D.   I, II, III and IV

28) Of the following treatment types or settings, which generally   28. _____
involves the highest improvement rate in nonbehavioral marital and family therapy?

A.   Individual
B.   Conjoint
C.   Conjoint group
D.   Concurrent

29) A therapist asks a husband and wife to consider their own   29. _____
behaviors during an interaction that has just taken place. The intervention
proceeded as follows:

Therapist: Can each of you tell me what happened in that last interaction?
Husband: "I know I'm sometimes overcritical."
Wife: "I guess I did something to annoy him."

Which of the following is true?

A.   the wife did not share the same level of responsibility as the husband
B.   the therapist's question appeared to favor one partner over the other
C.   the partners formed different interpretations of the question
D.   the therapist appears to have elicited a balanced response

30) According to the MRI model, all communication consists of the   30. _____
levels or functions of

A.   report and command
B.   receiver and sender
C.   verbal and nonverbal
D.   interrogative and declarative

31) What type of family coalition is represented in the diagram below?   31. _____

A.   Disengaged
B.   Skewed
C.   Generation gap
D.   Schismatic

32)   A couple and their two children are referred to a family therapist   32. _____
to seek help for strained relations between the father and mother. The father
and mother admit to treating each other badly, but both claim that all of their
disputes arise from discussions about how to deal with their troubled 14-year-old son.
From a structural perspective, this is an example of

A.   triangulation
B.   an idiosyncratic rule
C.   enactment
D.   a detouring coalition

33)   Regarding client task assignments, Strong and Claiborn named   33. _____
three principles that are useful in increasing spontaneous compliance. Which of
the following is not one of these?

A.   Personalism
B.   Incentive
C.   Choice
D.   Level of explicitness

34)   According to Haley, the family therapist should do each of the   34. _____
following, except

A.   modify the presenting problem through small, intermediate goals
B.   use empirical formulas to devise tasks and directives
C.   use the family value structure and culture to devise effective tasks
D.   assume that the feelings of family members are irrelevant to altering the presenting
problem

35)   In strategic family therapy, a therapist may sometimes attempt to   35. _____
overcome resistance by suggesting that a family not change, but continue
their interactive patterns. This method is known as

A.   intensity
B.   scapegoating
C.   extinction
D.   restraining

36)   According to Satir, family therapy should   36. _____

I.   recognize and incorporate individual uniqueness into decision making
II.   enhance individual expression of affect, behavior, and opinion among
family members
III.   encourage continued growth toward individual uniqueness
IV.   encourage the process of self-differentiation

A.   I and II
B.   I, II and III
C.   II, III, and IV
D.   I, II, III and IV

37) A family has been in therapy for several weeks. Attempts at out-of-session homework have failed repeatedly and the in-office sessions are stalled. It is probably an appropriate time for the therapist to

37. _____

A. issue an ultimatum for task completion
B. ask the family members to explain their resistance
C. discontinue therapy for a short period of time
D. try some paradoxical techniques

38) When asked to explain her tendency to demonstrate controlling behavior, a mother says to her daughter, "I just do it because I care so much about you." Of the four methods of destructive linear attribution identified by Strong and Claiborn, the mother is practicing

38. _____

A. debilitation
B. justification
C. rationalization
D. vilification

39) If the presenting problem for a family in therapy is a child's behavior, a behavioral therapist assumes the cause to be

39. _____

A. peer pressure
B. parenting skills
C. an unbalanced coalition
D. distress

40) During an intake interview, a therapist makes the decision to severely curtail the gathering of past family history, and instead focus on current interactions. Probably the greatest risk involved in this approach is that

40. _____

A. the heightened sense of emotional involvement might overwhelm family members
B. clients may begin to doubt the competency of the therapist
C. clients may become confused about the therapist's purpose
D. a lower degree of authenticity in client interactions

41) During a therapy session with a family of four, it is revealed that sometimes, when the father is not in the room, the mother describes some of the inadequacies in his parenting to the children, aged 8 and 11. From the perspective of the contextual model, the mother's actions indicate

41. _____

A. triangulation
B. diffuse boundaries
C. split filial loyalty
D. enmeshment

42) During the evaluative phase of a conjoint treatment program, the therapist should be careful about how he or she asks clients to explain the problem. Which of the following questions is most appropriately worded for this purpose?

42. _____

A. What is your theory about the problem?
B. What is the cause of this problem?
C. Where does this problem come from?
D. What do you think the problem is?

43) The experiential model assumes that change within a family requires 43. _____

A. a step backward or a temporary loss in functioning
B. the alteration of environmental contingencies
C. the addition of information to the family system
D. the introduction of new behavioral sequences

44) In the McMaster model of family evaluation, the intake interviewer 44. _____ attempts to maintain the focus as much as possible on the

A. past difficulties
B. identified patient
C. current family problem
D. parental coalition

45) Which of the following statements about structural family 45. _____ therapy is false?

A. The goal of therapy is to change boundaries and hierarchies.
B. The therapist assesses where in the system the structure fails to carry out its function.
C. In-session tasks focus on reinforcing existing patterns.
D. The therapist alters patterns by giving directives and demanding participation by the family members

46) Which of the following guidelines should be followed by a 46. _____ therapist in practice?

I. Clients should be informed clearly with an advance cancellation notice of at least 24 hours.
II. If a client misses an appointment, the therapist should charge the client and set up another time to meet.
III. If clients show up late to a meeting, they should be met for the entire therapeutic session and assessed a pro-rated charge.
IV. If two clients are inadvertently scheduled for the same time, the therapist should make up the session for one client and not charge for that session.

A. I only
B. I, II and IV
C. I and IV
D. I, II, III and IV

47) According to Minuchin, a person in a family with blurred 47. _____ psychological boundaries may experience a loss of autonomy known as

A. fusion
B. transference
C. enmeshment
D. undifferentiated ego mass

48) Of the following assessment instruments, which is probably most appropriate for measuring a family's problem-solving skills?   48. _____

A. Family Assessment Device (FAD)
B. Family Cohesion and Adaptability Evaluation Scale (FACES)
C. Dyadic Adjustment Scale (DAS)
D. Family Assessment Measure (FAM)

49) Each of the following is a technique commonly used by strategic family therapists, except   49. _____

A. Ordeals
B. Circular questioning
C. Reframing
D. Manipulating the symptom

50) Which of the following is not a technique commonly associated with Gestalt-experiential family therapy?   50. _____

A. establishing "ground rules"
B. the "empty chair" scenario
C. family sculpting
D. role-playing scenes from childhood

KEY (CORRECT ANSWERS)

1.	A		41.	C
2.	B		42.	A
3.	A		43.	A
4.	A		44.	C
5.	B		45.	C
6.	B		46.	B
7.	A		47.	C
8.	D		48.	A
9.	B		49.	B
10.	B		50.	C
11.	C			
12.	B			
13.	D			
14.	B			
15.	D			
16.	D			
17.	B			
18.	A			
19.	D			
20.	A			
21.	B			
22.	B			
23.	A			
24.	A			
25.	C			
26.	D			
27.	C			
28.	B			
29.	A			
30.	A			
31.	C			
32.	D			
33.	B			
34.	B			
35.	D			
36.	B			
37.	D			
38.	C			
39.	B			
40.	A			

TEST 2

Directions: Each question or incomplete statement is followed by several suggested answers or completions. Select the one the BEST answers the question or completes the statement. *PRINT THE LETTER OF THE CORRECT ANSWER IN THE SPACE AT THE RIGHT.*

1) Which of the following is a tactical skill that may be used in session by a therapist?

1. _____

A. Language
B. Humor
C. Self-disclosure
D. Self-confidence

2) In strategic family therapy, the therapist may sometimes instruct family members to continue their symptomatic behaviors. This is a method known as

2. _____

A. paradoxical directive
B. intensity
C. counterintuition
D. impact therapy

3) In the intensive, crisis-oriented form of family therapy developed by Robert MacGregor, family members are treated in various subgroups by a team of therapists. This method is known as

3. _____

A. multiple impact therapy
B. projective identification
C. multiple family therapy
D. instrumental structural therapy

4) Which of the following are elements of a treatment program in the Milan approach to family therapy?

4. _____

I. Sessions observed by a second therapy team
II. The main intervention usually involves role-playing
III. Families are asked to change immediately
IV. Limited to about 10 sessions

A. I only
B. I and IV
C. II only
D. II and III

5)   A couple that is described as "parallel" is defined as one in   5. _____
which the partners share a fear of

A.   rejection
B.   feelings
C.   exposure
D.   dependency

6)   Cognitive behavioral therapy identifies five types of cognitions   6. _____
that are applicable to intimate relationships. Which of the following is not one of these?

A.   Attributions
B.   Selective attention
C.   Summations
D.   Expectancies

7)   What type of boundary-breaking coalition is most likely to be   7. _____
present in severely disturbed families?

A.   Mother-daughter
B.   Mother-son
C.   Father-daughter
D.   Father-son

8)   Which of the following theorists is most closely associated with   8. _____
the concepts of power and control?

A.   Freud
B.   Haley
C.   Bowen
D.   Minuchin

9)   During a conflict resolution program with a married couple, a   9. _____
therapist begins to assess the function of the conflict in their relationship,
and picks up cues that the husband's anger is historically based. The most
appropriate next step would be to

A.   explore the husband's family of origin
B.   lay out the basic elements of the current conflict
C.   initiate communication training
D.   split the partners and treat them separately, focusing on the husband's unresolved
feelings

10)   The final stage of symbolic-experiential family therapy is   10. _____
referred to as

A.   denouement
B.   disentanglement
C.   integration
D.   uncoupling

11) A couple has developed an unconscious contract which the therapist believes is based on healthy needs and emphasizes a trading-off of needs, wants, and desires. The contract could be described as

11. _____

A. parallel
B. complementary
C. homeostatic
D. congruent

12) Which of the following is not a method commonly used by a family therapist to raise the intensity of therapeutic sessions?

12. _____

A. Using temporal or physical distance to reinforce boundaries
B. Altering the symptom
C. Enactments
D. Discouraging spontaneous behavior sequences

13) In the evaluation phase of any conjoint therapy program, most questions from individual partners should be

13. _____

A. answered as thoroughly as possible
B. directed back at the other partner
C. viewed with skepticism
D. ignored

14) A family is in therapy, in part to treat the drinking problem of their adolescent son. The father believes the son drinks because he is insecure. This explanation can be described as

14. _____

A. dyadic
B. triadic
C. quadratic
D. monadic

15) What is another term for the Milan approach to family therapy?

15. _____

A. Narrative
B. Symbolic
C. Experiential
D. Systemic

16) During a series of conjoint sessions, while observing the interactions of a husband and wife, a therapist finds himself continually and silently in agreement with the wife's viewpoint. This is probably a sign that

16. _____

A. the husband's behavior is the most likely cause of the problem
B. the wife is a more accomplished arguer than the husband
C. the therapist's interpretations are free of gender bias
D. the therapist is experiencing countertransference and should undergo personal therapy

17)   A therapist responds to an argument between a husband and   17. _____
wife by saying, "The two of you must care a great deal for each other,
if you invest so much of your energy in fighting." This is an example of

A.   exaggerating a cognitive distortion
B.   interpretation
C.   denial
D.   reframing

18)   A therapist uses psychoeducational family therapy for a family   18. _____
with a schizophrenic member. After the hospital release and initial intervention,
which of the following should be used next to reduce the chance of a relapse?

A.   Structural and behavioral therapy
B.   Solution-focused therapy
C.   Externalization and MRI
D.   Strategic therapy

19)   A family therapist who acts as a facilitator and clarifier of family   19. _____
interaction, rather than being directive, is described as a(n)

A.   promoter
B.   conductor
C.   balancer
D.   reactor

20)   According to Madanes, all problems presented to therapy result   20. _____
from the dilemma between

A.   independence and dependence
B.   attraction and repulsion
C.   sex and love
D.   love and violence

21)   Each of the following is a common purpose of reframing, except   21. _____

A.   changing the attribution of a symptom from bad to good
B.   changing motivations from selfish to generous
C.   moving the focus from the individual to the system
D.   changing attributions from linear to circular

22)   In behavioral therapy, a stimulus which differentially produces one   22. _____
of a number of possible responses is described as

A.   focused
B.   transmissive
C.   discriminating
D.   reinforcing

23) Family therapists sometimes make use of a nonverbal experiential   23. _____
technique in which family members position themselves in a physical
arrangement that reveals significant aspects of their perceptions and feelings.
This technique is known as

A. genography
B. sculpting
C. role-playing
D. scripting

24) During therapy, a therapist discovers the following pattern to be   24. _____
typical between a parent and child: the parent makes a request, the child
makes an aversive response, and the parent acquiesces. In the behavioral
model, this is an example of

A. a symmetrical relationship
B. reciprocity
C. negative reinforcement
D. a coercive interaction

25) Of the following, which should probably take place first during   25. _____
an intake interview with clients?

A. Developmental history
B. Statement of presenting problem
C. Initial intervention
D. Cross-sectional history

26) During a session, which of the following should most likely   26. _____
be discouraged as a sentence spoken by one spouse to another?

A. "Dr. _____ said you shouldn't talk to me like that."
B. "She doesn't follow through with her ambitions."
C. "I wonder if I've been attentive enough to you."
D. "I don't know why you talk to me like that."

27) Proponents of the MRI model of family therapy include each of   27. _____
the following, except

A. Watzlawick
B. Boszoremenyi-Nagy
C. Bateson
D. Jackson

28) The idea that relative birth order is a significant factor in   28. _____
determining specific characteristics is an element of the _____ model.

A. Bowen systems
B. structural
C. experiential
D. behavioral

29)   A family composed of a couple and their children, a 12-year-old   29. _____
boy and a 15-year-old girl, attends weekly therapy sessions. During many
sessions, the therapist observes that whenever the father begins to speak to
or about the son in a manner that is critical or negative, the daughter joins in,
listing the boy's record of recent misbehavior. The father seems to accept her input
approvingly. Most likely, this is an example of

A.   a cross-generational coalition
B.   pseudomutuality
C.   a double-bind
D.   projective identification

30)   In the early phase of conjoint couple treatment, the therapist's   30. _____
job is typically to _____ affect.

A.   manage
B.   intensify
C.   ignore
D.   manipulate

31)   In Bowen systems therapy,   31. _____

A.   the therapist is authoritative and directive
B.   the goal is to separate intellectual from emotional functioning
C.   dyads are considered to be the most stable form of family subsystem
D.   emotional illness is believed to be the result of cumulative traumas inflicted by early
caregivers

32)   What is the term for the primitive form of identification in which a   32. _____
person takes in aspects of other people to form parts of his or her self-image?

A.   Individuation
B.   Undifferentiation
C.   Introjection
D.   Mystification

33)   In couple therapy, the most common presentation by each   33. _____
partner is to

A.   deny that a problem exists
B.   accept an undue amount of responsibility for the presenting problem
C.   project one's own dysfunctional qualities onto the other
D.   place blame and responsibility on the other partner

34)   Phase 3 of a psychoeducational treatment program typically includes

A.   allowing family members access to treatment team members   34. _____
between sessions
B.   redirecting families who have achieved the basic contract
C.   assessing stressors
D.   teaching communication skills training

35) Contingency contracting of most likely a component of a treatment program in the _____ model of family therapy.

35. _____

A. narrative
B. behavioral
C. structural
D. systemic

36) The ultimate goal of strategic family therapy can be said to be

36. _____

A. eliminating helplessness
B. removing the presenting problem
C. maximizing emotional expression
D. redefining the family hierarchy

37) According to Feldman, the underlying cause of marital conflict is

37. _____

A. historical and residual anger
B. cognitive distortion
C. introjection
D. narcissistic vulnerability

38) In the later stages of its development, behavioral family therapy has tended to increase the importance of

38. _____

A. cognitions and attributions
B. contingency contracting
C. feeling statements
D. anger management

39) One of the primary goals during the evaluation phase of a conjoint treatment program is to

39. _____

A. assess covert messages
B. identify a problem's historical roots
C. normalize differences
D. intensify emotions

40) During a heated in-session exchange, a therapist interrupts an arguing couple and says, "You know, I don't like either of you!" What type of intervention is this?

40. _____

A. Strategic
B. Scripted
C. Behavioral
D. Experiential

41) The therapeutic technique of enactment is designed to produce each of the following outcomes, except

41. _____

A. destabilizing the family system
B. lowering in-session intensity
C. providing the therapist with information about the family structure
D. providing the therapist with an opportunity for a reframe

42)   A therapist wants to describe the concept of effective boundaries   42. _____
for a couple, but wants to avoid professional jargon. She decides upon the
use of an analogy. Which of the following is most suitable?

A.   Fences with gates that are opened and closed from the inside.
B.   A green light.
C.   A child experimenting with finger paints.
D.   A castle with a moat but no drawbridge.

43)   According to Bowen, emotionally fused individuals   43. _____

A.   demonstrate adaptation in family relationships
B.   possess a solid and genuine self
C.   use emotions of self and others as a guide
D.   transcend individual and familial emotions

44)   Which of the following theories involve the concept of   44. _____
diffuse boundaries?

A.   Structural and object relations
B.   Strategic and experiential
C.   Experiential and structural
D.   Ordeal and object relations

45)   Which of the following theories explains relationships in terms of   45. _____
costs and benefits?

A.   Behavior exchange theory
B.   Structural theory
C.   General systems theory
D.   Network theory

46)   Which of the following is an example of a "linear" question?   46. _____

A.   Does anyone else in your family often feel sad?
B.   What role do your moods play in your interactions with your children?
C.   Do you think your sadness might be related to the way your wife responds to you?
D.   Why are you so sad?

47)   During a session with a husband and wife, the wife begins to   47. _____
weep uncontrollably. The therapist asks, "What are your early memories
about crying as hard as you are right now?" This is a strategy known as

A.   the holding environment
B.   object relations
C.   interpretation
D.   transference

48) Which of the following is typically performed at the latest stage in communication training?

48. _____

A. Feedback
B. Reinforcement
C. Homework
D. Modeling

49) Stressors that are transmitted to family members through previous generations are described as

49. _____

A. subliminal
B. vertical
C. transverse
D. horizontal

50) In general, each of the following is a guideline for the therapist to follow in treating couples, except

50. _____

A. If the therapist sees the wife for an individual session in the initial stage of therapy, the husband should also be seen separately.
B. Individual therapy should never be allowed to evolve into couple therapy--it should result in a referral.
C. If individual sessions are considered necessary to break up emotional blocks or enmeshment, the number of individual sessions should be roughly equal for each partner.
D. If only one individual appears for a session when both partners were supposed to be present, the therapist should schedule an individual visit for the other partner soon in the future.

KEY (CORRECT ANSWERS)

1.	A	41.	B
2.	A	42.	A
3.	A	43.	C
4.	B	44.	A
5.	D	45.	A
6.	C	46.	D
7.	B	47.	C
8.	B	48.	C
9.	A	49.	B
10.	B	50.	B
11.	D		
12.	D		
13.	C		
14.	D		
15.	D		
16.	D		
17.	D		
18.	A		
19.	D		
20.	D		
21.	B		
22.	C		
23.	B		
24.	D		
25.	B		
26.	A		
27.	B		
28.	A		
29.	A		
30.	A		
31.	B		
32.	C		
33.	D		
34.	A		
35.	B		
36.	B		
37.	D		
38.	A		
39.	C		
40.	D		

TEST 3

Directions: Each question or incomplete statement is followed by several suggested answers or completions. Select the one the BEST answers the question or completes the statement. *PRINT THE LETTER OF THE CORRECT ANSWER IN THE SPACE AT THE RIGHT.*

1) A therapist must obtain written informed consent from a client before

    1. _____

    I.   transcribing the words of a client into a notepad
    II.   making an audio recording of a session
    III. videotaping a session
    IV. having a third party observe the session

A.   I, II and III
B.   II and III only
C.   II, III and IV
D.   I, II, III and IV

2) During a particular session, a 37-year-old male client expresses a deepening anger with a former girlfriend who is now dating the client's former friend. The client states that if she doesn't end the relationship with the former friend, he will kill her--and he provides a detailed plan for doing so. What should the therapist do?

    2. _____

A.   Respect the client's privacy and try to talk him out of his plan.
B.   Tell the police and the former girlfriend.
C.   Advise the client against it, and then wait to see if his anger lasts until the next session.
D.   Tell the former girlfriend and former friend.

3) A client states that she does not feel very intelligent or capable. This is a problem that should probably be addressed from the _____ perspective.

    3. _____

A.   behavioral
B.   structural
C.   object relations
D.   cognitive

4)   The Bowenian genogram below denotes   4. _____

A.   a birth
B.   an abortion
C.   a marital separation
D.   a divorce

5)   The insight-awareness model of has also been known as each of   5. _____
the following, <u>except</u>

A.   psychoanalytic
B.   historical
C.   psychodynamic
D.   psychoeducational

6)   A therapist establishes a system of rewards for a family that uses   6. _____
points, which can be accumulated or exchanged for reinforcing items or
behaviors. This is an example of

A.   social learning
B.   a subsystem
C.   a token economy
D.   hierarchical structure

7)   According to the structural model, which of the following is <u>not</u> a   7. _____
valid assumption to make about a symptom?

A.   It deflects intrasubsystem conflict onto a scapegoat
B.   It signals a structural deficit.
C.   It focuses attention on the subsystem where it exists
D.   It retards normal developmental maturation

8)   Which of the following models of family therapy is associated with   8. _____
the "3-S pot"?

A.   Behavioral
B.   Satir
C.   Ordeal
D.   Structural

9)   Some behavioral sex therapies begin by teaching couples   9. _____
to employ sexual pleasuring without the pressure to actually engage
in intercourse. This is known as

A.   delayed gratification
B.   sensate focus
C.   tension-building
D.   the squeeze technique

10)   The goal of _____ family therapy is to achieve an   10. _____
integrated view of reality through accepting repressed and forgotten memories.

A.   solution-focused
B.   psychoeducational
C.   Bowen systems
D.   object relations

11)   In the coaching model, the major strategy in reducing family   11. _____
resistance to therapy is

A.   confrontation
B.   psychoeducation
C.   paradoxical techniques
D.   rationale and positive reinforcement

12)   What is term in family therapy commonly used to describe a   12. _____
step-family?

A.   Blended
B.   Differentiated
C.   Reconstituted
D.   Re-engaged

13)   In the "ABCD" model of Ellis's rational-emotive therapy, B is   13. _____
commonly referred to as

A.   a person's self-statement
B.   an action or event that can be observed
C.   the thought that motivated an action
D.   a marital dispute

14)   A family presents to a therapists with an 8-year-old daughter who   14. _____
suffers from chronic bed-wetting. With the therapist's help, the family
reconstructs the bed-wetting occasions as a visit from a mischievous creature
known as the Puddlejumper. The family then discusses ways in which they can come
together in their struggle against the Puddlejumper. This is an example of the
_____ approach to family therapy.

A.   Bowen systems
B.   narrative
C.   object relations
D.   experiential

15) In the clinical application of the "triangle" model of love in marital therapy, which of the following questions should be asked <u>first</u>?

15. _____

A. Whether both partners desire all three components of the triangle
B. Whether each partner has realistic perceptions of what love involves
C. What prevents the identification and expression of the three components
D. Whether each partner wants the same intensity for each component

16) Behavioral observations make in a laboratory setting are sometimes referred to as _____ observations.

16. _____

A. anecdotal
B. naturalistic
C. simulated
D. analog

17) Which of the following family treatment techniques is most likely to pay significant attention to nonverbal behaviors?

17. _____

A. Bibliotherapy
B. Behavioral interventions
C. Gestalt techniques
D. Guided fantasy

18) In general, an introject can be detected by

18. _____

    I. a trained therapist
    II. other family members
    III. third-party observers
    IV. the symptom bearer

A. I only
B. I and III
C. II and IV
D. I, II, III and IV

19) A couple in conjoint therapy tell the therapist that every time they talk, they end up arguing. This is a problem that would benefit most from the application of principles in the _____ approach.

19. _____

A. Communication
B. Narrative
C. Contextual
D. Behavioral

20) Which of the following assessment instruments is exclusively self-reported?

20. _____

A. Dyadic Adjustment Scale (DAS)
B. Marital Observation Checklist (MOC)
C. Marital Interaction Coding System (MICS)
D. Marital Satisfaction Time Line (MSTL)

21)   The symbol below is used by structural family therapists   21. _____
to denote

A.   a clear boundary
B.   involvement
C.   a rigid boundary
D.   overinvolvement

22)   The "settling down" period in a marital relationship is typical   22. _____
of couples in the _____ age group.

A.   22-28
B.   29-31
C.   32-39
D.   40-42

23)   The concepts of boundaries and hierarchies are most closely   23. _____
associated with the ideas of

A.   Bateson
B.   Haley
C.   Minuchin
D.   Bowen

24)   Phase 1 of a psychoeducational treatment program typically   24. _____
includes

A.   limit testing
B.   identifying minimal rules that satisfy each member of the family
C.   focusing on social and work domains
D.   devising a contract containing mutual, attainable, and specific goals

25)   The major techniques associated with solution-focused family   25. _____
therapy include each of the following, except

A.   exceptions
B.   scaling
C.   the pretend technique
D.   the miracle question

26)   Each of the following theorists has worked from the assumption   26. _____
that previous generations influence a person's current functioning, except

A.   Framo
B.   Selvini-Palazzoli
C.   Boszormenyi-Nagy
D.   Bowen

27)   In some families, a blurring of psychological boundaries between   27. _____
self and others can occur that impairs emotional and intellectual functioning.
This phenomenon is known to structural therapists as

A.   individuation
B.   fusion
C.   blending
D.   differentiation

28)   After a few sessions of therapy, a married couple is able to observe 28. _____
and comment on patterns of behavior--for example, the husband says, "You
attacked me and then I got defensive, and then you attacked again and I got
even more defensive." In terms of the schema proposed by Bernal and Barker,
this couple has achieved communication at the _____ level.

A.   Relational
B.   Individual
C.   Transactional
D.   Contextual

29)   In which of the following models is the therapist   29. _____
generally nondirective?

A.   Behavioral
B.   Strategic
C.   Object relations
D.   Structural

30)   Each of the following is a potential drawback associated with   30. _____
the use of individual sessions in conjoint therapy, except

A.   the appearance of labeling one partner as the "sick one"
B.   the alignment of one partner and the therapist
C.   the revelation of secrets
D.   unknowingly splitting the couple into separate paths of individual growth

31)   The rationale behind the technique of symptom practicing in   31. _____
therapy is to

A.   elucidate the problems associated with the symptom
B.   imply the ability to control the symptom
C.   weaken the powers associated with the symptom
D.   create an aversion to the symptom

32)   During a conjoint session, a wife says to her husband, "The only   32. _____
reason you come on to me right at the end of the work day is because you
know I'm tired and not in the mood. You want me to turn you down so you
can use it against me later." Of the four methods of destructive linear attribution
identified by Strong and Claiborn, the wife is practicing

A.   debilitation
B.   justification
C.   rationalization
D.   vilification

33)　　The object relations model of family therapy assumes that　　33. _____
problems persist because families are in a process of unconscious collusion
in perpetuating the projective identification process. Each of the following is
considered to be an effect of this collusion, <u>except</u>

A.　　reduced anxiety in the person with the intrapsychic deficit
B.　　placement of the symptom-bearer in the most powerful place in each intrafamily
coalition
C.　　encouragement of cohesion within the family by providing a common concern or
focus
D.　　maintenance of self-esteem in the symptom-bearer, who serves a central role in the
family

34)　　When a person automatically uses a habitual pattern of thinking　　34. _____
in assessing a situation, the patterns often create what are known as

A.　　affective disorders
B.　　cognitive distortions
C.　　behavioral anomalies
D.　　mental set

35)　　In which of the following models of family therapy does the　　35. _____
therapist work to frame the problem as an outside entity, against which the
family must form a united front?

A.　　Narrative
B.　　Experiential
C.　　Milan approach
D.　　Solution-focused

36)　　Rubin's four main components of love include　　36. _____

　　　I.　　Caring
　　　II.　　Tolerance
　　　III.　　Trusting
　　　IV.　　Needing

A.　　I and II only
B.　　I, II and III
C.　　II and III only
D.　　I, II, III and IV

37)　　A therapist who uses high probability behavior to reinforce low　　37. _____
probability behavior is making use of

A.　　positive connotation
B.　　object relations
C.　　the Premack principle
D.　　extension

38)   Which of the following statements or questions, spoken from   38. _____
one spouse to another, is probably intended to establish intimacy?

A.   I feel as if I never get to see you any more.
B.   You don't act like you love me any more.
C.   You never spend time with me.
D.   I am really hurting inside.

39)   According to Bowen, which of the following statements about   39. _____
emotionally detached people is generally <u>false</u>?

A.   They use personal principles as a guide.
B.   They are less susceptible to influence by others.
C.   They demonstrate adaptation and independence in family relationships.
D.   They are less consistent in their decision-making over time.

40)   Of the following, the most significant problem associated with   40. _____
quid pro quo contracts in marital therapy is that

A.   they encompass a limited range of behaviors
B.   rewards are often hard to quantify
C.   they do not address the motivation for certain behaviors
D.   one partner must always perform first

41)   What is the term for the therapeutic technique by which the   41. _____
therapist appears similar to family members through imitation of body
language, style, and idiosyncrasy?

A.   Mimesis
B.   Enactment
C.   Projection
D.   Sculpting

42)   Techniques commonly used in emotion-focused couples   42. _____
therapy include

        I.   experiments in awareness
        II.   framing difficulties as underlying vulnerabilities
        III.   empathetic reflection
        IV.   adding pragmatic but seemingly inappropriate interventions

A.   I only
B.   I, II, and III
C.   II, III, and IV
D.   I, II, III and IV

43)   In extreme forms of distancing within families, some members   43. _____
withdraw physically or emotionally to cope with the anxiety inherent in the
defective family system. According to Bowen, the disadvantages to this extreme
withdrawal include

    I.   replication across generations
    II.   reduction in support available to the nuclear family
    III.   adoption of "black sheep" role
    IV.   greater susceptibility to outside influences

A.   I and II
B.   II and IV
C.   None of the above
D.   I, II, III and IV

44)   In an intersystem assessment for a married couple, which of the   44. _____
following is considered an element of the intergenerational system?

A.   Communication styles
B.   Defense mechanisms
C.   Boundaries
D.   Linear attributional strategies

45)   During which stage of a standard therapy session in the Milan   45. _____
approach does the team construct an intervention for the family?

A.   Presession
B.   Intercession
C.   Intervention
D.   Postsession

46)   During conjoint therapy, a husband continually reveals the   46. _____
thought--often apparently unconscious--that his wife should spend all of
her time with him. On occasions when the wife doesn't spend time with him,
the husband assumes she doesn't love him. From a cognitive perspective, one of the
therapist's tasks is to

A.   train the husband to become more comfortable with his wife's absence
B.   convince the wife to remain closer to the husband for a while
C.   expose the irrational thinking and the negative judgement made on the basis of it
D.   associate the wife's absence with a positive stimulus

47)   When a therapist has an unconscious emotional reaction to a   47. _____
patient or a member of a family in treatment, which of the following has occurred?

A.   Schism
B.   Enmeshment
C.   Projective identification
D.   Countertransference

48) A major disadvantage associated with the use of spouse-reported 48. _____
questionnaires as instruments of marital evaluation is

A. complex administration
B. lower cost-efficiency than other instruments
C. a higher level of reactivity and bias
D. behavioral data set

49) Some therapists believe that a client will attempt to reduce anxiety 49. _____
by isolating and repressing undesirable features of an early caregiver. This is known as

A. splitting
B. differentiation
C. inexpedience
D. schism

50) Each of the following is a type of cognitive distortion, <u>except</u> 50. _____

A. mental filter
B. either-or thinking
C. jumping to conclusions
D. disengagement

KEY (CORRECT ANSWERS)

1.	C	41.	A
2.	B	42.	B
3.	D	43.	A
4.	B	44.	C
5.	D	45.	B
6.	C	46.	C
7.	C	47.	D
8.	B	48.	C
9.	B	49.	A
10.	D	50.	D
11.	D		
12.	A		
13.	A		
14.	B		
15.	A		
16.	D		
17.	C		
18.	A		
19.	A		
20.	A		
21.	A		
22.	C		
23.	C		
24.	D		
25.	C		
26.	B		
27.	B		
28.	C		
29.	C		
30.	C		
31.	B		
32.	D		
33.	B		
34.	B		
35.	A		
36.	D		
37.	C		
38.	D		
39.	D		
40.	D		

EXAMINATION SECTION
TEST 1

Directions: Each question or incomplete statement is followed by several suggested answers or completions. Select the one the BEST answers the question or completes the statement. *PRINT THE LETTER OF THE CORRECT ANSWER IN THE SPACE AT THE RIGHT.*

1) Distorted emotional reactions to present relationships based on early family relations are often labeled with the psychoanalytic term

1. _____

A. dissociation
B. transference
C. projection
D. regression

2) What is Lidz's term for a pathological marriage in which one spouse dominates another?

2. _____

A. Marital skew
B. Marital governance
C. Marital schism
D. Marital asymmetry

3) Typically, in an initial session with a couple, chairs should be arranged in the following way:

3. _____

A. The couple should be seated alongside each other, facing the therapist.
B. The therapist should sit between the two partners.
C. The three chairs should be placed to equally face the other two, in an approximate triangle.
D. The couple should be facing each other a good distance from the therapist.

4) The theorist who devised the model known as contextual family therapy is

4. _____

A. Framo
B. Prata
C. Boszormenyi-Nagy
D. Bowen

5) During a conjoint marital session, a therapist may create or enhance intensity by

5. _____

I. Repeating what each partner says
II. Exaggerating the cognitive distortions of clients
III. Offering insights
IV. Posing questions intended to lead the client toward more depth of feeling

A. I only
B. I and II
C. II and III
D. II, III and IV

6) Which of the following models of family therapy requires   6. _____
clients to "process insight"?

A. Object relations
B. Structural
C. Cognitive behavioral
D. Experiential

7) The MRI model of family therapy assumes that similar events or   7. _____
inputs across individuals cannot be assumed to have similar effects. This concept is
referred to as

A. dynamism
B. equifinality
C. second-order change
D. equipotentiality

Questions 8 and 9 refer to the following information: A mother, father, and
their 12-year-old son attend regular therapy sessions to explore the son's fear
of going to school. The fear emerged after a trial separation between the mother
and father. The father moved back in after it became clear that the only way to get their son
to attend school would be for the father and mother to work together to help him.

8) From the perspective of Boszormenyi-Nagy, this situation reveals   8. _____
an example of

A. fusion
B. triangulation
C. individuation
D. invisible loyalties

9) From the behavioral perspective, the situation between the parents   9. _____
and their son is an example of

A. extinction
B. negative reinforcement
C. positive reinforcement
D. shaping

10) Which of the following approaches has/have roots in the MRI   10. _____
model of family therapy?

    I. The narrative approach
    II. The experiential approach
    III. The Milan approach
    IV. Solution-focused therapy

A. I and II
B. I, III and IV
C. II and IV
D. I, II, III and IV

11) In structural family therapy, a therapist may begin treatment by accepting and accommodating a family, in order to win their confidence and circumvent resistance. The name for this strategy is

11. _____

A. modeling
B. introjection
C. joining
D. projective identification

12) Which of the following should the therapist generally reserve for sessions occurring after the initial assessment sessions?

12. _____

A. Explanation and rationale for the treatment process
B. Restatement of each spouse's concerns
C. Notation of goals discusses
D. Comments on the client's interactional style

13) Which of the following is a position Family-of-Origin therapy?

13. _____

A. The attempt to fix small difficulties sometimes leads to larger problems
B. Emotional expression is a critical means for enhancing personal growth
C. Aberrant behavior reflects internal conflict
D. Problems reflect irrational role assignments

14) In the initial evaluation of a family or couple, a therapist faces "choice points" that are both substantive and technical. Which of the following is a technical choice point?

14. _____

A. Whether to focus on crisis or the general character of the family
B. Focusing on the family as the central shaping force or on the environment's influence on the family
C. How to "type" the family in standardized measurements
D. Whether to seek family "themes" or look at concrete behaviors

15) Which of the following is not considered to be a paradoxical therapeutic technique?

15. _____

A. Positioning
B. Manipulating the symptom
C. Prescribing the symptom
D. Restraining the change

16) According to the schema of Bernal and Barker, which of the following types of communication is considered to be most sophisticated and mature?

16. _____

A. Contextual
B. Transactional
C. Relational
D. Individual

17)   According to the AAMFT, therapists must refrain from sexual   17. _____
involvement with clients

A.   indefinitely, without regard to the date of termination
B.   until two years have passed since termination
C.   until six months have passed since termination
D.   only during the course of therapy

18)   The psychoeducational model of family therapy incorporates   18. _____
techniques from the _____ models.

A.   object relations and structural
B.   narrative and experiential
C.   strategic and functional
D.   structural and behavioral

319)   During a conjoint marital therapy session, the wife, Joan, states   19. _____
that she feels as if she and her husband don't go out together as much as
they used to. The husband, Carl, responds by saying he's tired of hearing
her complain all the time, and that she reminds him of a man named Jim, whom
he works with, who also complains all the time. Carl talks for several minutes
about how difficult work is because of people like Jim. Most likely, the therapist
should follow this up with words such as

A.   Let's return to the subject, please.
B.   Joan, what happens when you bring up this kind of conversation at home?
C.   Carl, I'd like to hear more about your troubles at work.
D.   What does that have to do with anything?

20)   Of the following functions of anger in a relationship, the one   20. _____
that is probably healthiest is

A.   signaling boundary violations
B.   asserting power and control
C.   regulating distance
D.   testing the degree of commitment

21)   During the problem stage of a strategic treatment program, the   21. _____
therapist should

A.   focus on the present situation rather than the history behind it
B.   become actively involved in identifying the problem
C.   ask about the feelings of family members
D.   offer comments on the client's perspective of the problem

22)   From the therapist's perspective, which of the following   22. _____
"disguises" for anger is typically most difficult to detect?

A.   Self-victimization
B.   The tactic of reason and rationality
C.   The adoption of righteousness
D.   Passive-aggressive behavior

23)   According to Bion, group members become diverted from the   23. _____
group task to pursue certain unconscious patterns. Which of the following
such patterns is not named by Bion's basic assumption theory?

A.   Dependency
B.   Shaping
C.   Pairing
D.   Fight-flight

24)   Of the four "octaves" of therapeutic skills described by Bugental,   24. _____
the one most likely to be implemented at a later stage in therapy is

A.   guiding and focusing
B.   requiring or confronting
C.   instructing and teaching
D.   listening

25)   Interventions in behavioral family therapy typically have four   25. _____
components. Which of the following is not one of these?

A.   Evaluation of the intervention
B.   Enactment of projected extinction
C.   Construction of hypothesized relationships among relevant variables
D.   Data collection via observation

26)   In most severely disturbed families, the parental coalition is   26. _____
likely to be described as

A.   absent
B.   weak
C.   inconsistent
D.   flexible

27)   A therapist working in the MRI model encounters a client who is   27. _____
overcome with stage fright. Most likely, this therapist would instruct to client to

A.   identify the disadvantages of improvement
B.   explore early memories associated with this fear
C.   implement a daily practice routine
D.   try harder to relax when onstage

28)   Toward the end of a work day, a husband shows up on time for   28. _____
a marital therapy session, but the wife has called on her cell phone to let the
therapist know she is stuck in traffic and will be several minutes late. The
therapist says he has a few errands to run while they wait, and leaves the husband
alone in the office until the wife arrives. In this case, the therapist has attempted to protect
himself against

A.   triangulation
B.   projective identification
C.   litigation
D.   countertransference

29) Which of the following assumptions remains a cornerstone of   29. _____
the structural model of family therapy?

A.   Only the behaviors of family members at the top of the family hierarchies influence
and reflect family structure.
B.   Therapy focuses on existing patterns and maintaining existing hierarchies while
changing specific behaviors.
C.   The optimal family structure has rigid boundaries.
D.   The presenting problem has a homeostatic function.

30)   A client states that he has generally negative attitudes, but he   30. _____
doesn't know where he gets them. Which of the following approaches
would be most useful in addressing this problem?

A.   Structural
B.   Narrative
C.   Communication
D.   Contextual

31)   What is the term for the unconscious process by which a mate or   31. _____
offspring unwittingly assumes another person's undesirable internalized features?

A.   Cleaving
B.   Transference
C.   Internal duplication
D.   Projective identification

32)   In a typical family evaluation, the first step is most likely to be   32. _____

A.   formulating family problem areas
B.   determining the current phase of the family life cycle
C.   planning the therapeutic approach
D.   recording explicit interview data

33)   The Milan approach to family therapy makes use of a technique in   33. _____
which beneficial and constructive motives are ascribed to family behaviors,
in order to promote cohesion and to decrease resistance to therapy. This technique
is known as

A.   constructive deception
B.   pretend technique
C.   positive connotation
D.   joining

34) In most marital and family treatment programs, the therapist needs 34. _____
to facilitate communication that moves from

    I.   linear to circular
    II.   intent to effect
    III.   content to process
    IV.   contextual to relational

A.   I only
B.   I and III
C.   II and IV
D.   I, II, III and IV

35) When not making a specific interaction during couple therapy, 35. _____
the general body position of the therapist should be

A.   toward the middle of the space between the clients
B.   reclined so as not to suggest favoring one over the other
C.   deflected to the side, away from both clients
D.   toward the person who is speaking

36) Which of the following is a process that teaches a couple or family 36. _____
how to turn vague, global and generalized statements of relationship satisfaction
into well-specified descriptions of pleasing and displeasing behavior?

A.   Differentiation
B.   Self-summary
C.   Objectification
D.   Behavioral exchange

37) A young couple and their 4-year-old daughter are referred to a 37. _____
therapist to seek a solution to their daughter's inexplicable aggression toward
other children. During the first few sessions, the couple report that they have a
marriage that is relatively free of troubles--but during these sessions they seem
overly cautious about contradicting each other. A structural therapist would probably
conclude that these sessions indicate an underlying situation of

A.   rigidity
B.   fusion
C.   marital discord
D.   inadequate boundaries

38) When working individually with a client whose difficulties are 38. _____
centered on his or her role in a family, it is usually best to address personal issues

A.   systemically
B.   structurally
C.   from an object relations perspective
D.   narratively

39) The ultimate goal of psychoeducational family therapy is to   39. _____

A. eliminate the chance of schizophrenic relapse
B. simulate a protective isolation
C. delay relapse
D. enhance the client's emotional experience

40) Which of the following types of family therapies uses treatment   40. _____
that consists of a multicouples group format?

A. Bowen systems
B. Family-of-Origin
C. Milan
D. Contextual

41) Marriages are sometimes classified according to their level of   41. _____
intimacy. In this typology, the "passive-congenial" marriage

A. is pleasant and involves the sharing of interests, but there is not great intensity of
interaction
B. intensely satisfying to the spouses in at least one major area
C. involves covert expressions of satisfaction, with partners conducting separate lives
in many areas
D. is characterized by severe conflicts, but the partners are held together by fear of
alternatives

42) In behavioral therapy, the attempt to eliminate undesirable   42. _____
behaviors through non-reinforcement is known as

A. disassociation
B. negative reinforcement
C. shaping
D. extinction

43) During a marital therapy session, a therapist interrupts an   43. _____
argument by saying, "I won't let you do this." This is an example of
managing intensity through

A. stronger confrontation
B. changing the structure of the discussion
C. emotional intervention
D. process questions

44) In order to help a couple with their communication problems, it is   44. _____
typically most useful for the therapist to first work with them in learning to
differentiate between

A. sender and recipient
B. intent and effect
C. cognition and affect
D. content and process

45) When an enactment is being structured by a therapist during a   45. _____
couple session, the most appropriate thing for the therapist to do with his/her eyes is

A.   look down and avoid eye contact
B.   focus on the person who happens to be speaking
C.   focus on the partner who is the identified patient
D.   look constantly back and forth between the two clients

46) The idea that repressed impulses and unexpressed emotions are the 46. _____
cause of psychological dysfunction is the cornerstone of _____ family therapy.

A.   object relations
B.   experiential
C.   narrative
D.   Bowenian

47) A therapist begins working with a couple in conjoint therapy to   47. _____
prepare a written marital contract. The couple is resistant to put the contract
in writing--it seems so cold and legalistic, they say--and ask the therapist to
explain why it has to be written down. The therapist's response could include
each of the following, except

A.   it will make it more difficult to forget or distort the agreement if it is written down
B.   it will server as a constant reminder of the couple's commitment to each other
C.   all important events--births, deaths and events of significant progress--are
documented, and the beginning of this new agreement is just as important
D.   it can be used as irrefutable proof that one partner has violated a specific section of
the agreement

48) Stressors that are produced by a family as they move through   48. _____
the transitions of the family life cycle are described as

A.   horizontal
B.   calendrical
C.   vertical
D.   transformational

49) In the conflict model, the major strategy in reducing family   49. _____
resistance to therapy is

A.   object-focused techniques
B.   encouragement and rationale
C.   paradoxical techniques
D.   confrontation and interpretation

50) During the initial therapy sessions with a married couple, a female therapist
encounters a great deal of overt hostility from the husband. After several sessions, the
therapist begins to form the opinion that she somehow reminds the husband of his mother.
His behavior is an example of

A.   transference
B.   self-fulfilling assumption
C.   projective identification
D.   a derivative

KEY (CORRECT ANSWERS)

1.	B		41.	A
2.	A		42.	D
3.	C		43.	A
4.	C		44.	B
5.	B		45.	A
6.	A		46.	B
7.	D		47.	D
8.	D		48.	A
9.	C		49.	D
10.	B		50.	A
11.	C			
12.	A			
13.	D			
14.	C			
15.	B			
16.	A			
17.	B			
18.	D			
19.	B			
20.	A			
21.	A			
22.	B			
23.	B			
24.	B			
25.	B			
26.	A			
27.	A			
28.	D			
29.	D			
30.	D			
31.	D			
32.	B			
33.	C			
34.	B			
35.	A			
36.	C			
37.	C			
38.	A			
39.	C			
40.	B			

TEST 2

Directions: Each question or incomplete statement is followed by several suggested answers or completions. Select the one the BEST answers the question or completes the statement. *PRINT THE LETTER OF THE CORRECT ANSWER IN THE SPACE AT THE RIGHT.*

1) With their therapist, a couple develops a contract that includes the following agreement: if Bill wants Maria to go antiquing with him on Saturday and she decides to join him, she chooses a reward she would like, such as spending a night out with her friends. This is an example of a _____ contract.

1. _____

A. covenant
B. quid pro quo
C. contingent
D. good faith

2) Of the following family therapy models, which tends to view unexpressed emotion as an impediment to functioning?

2. _____

A. Symbolic-experiential
B. Psychoeducational
C. Structural
D. Bowen systems

3) During the course of treatment, a therapist has several objective means by which he or she may assess the level of professional balance or bias. Which of the following is not one of these?

3. _____

A. Monitoring the time spent on each client.
B. Switching to equally-timed sessions of individual therapy.
C. Counting the interchanges between clients.
D. Making direct inquiries to clients about their perceptions.

4) Which of the following is a closed-ended question?

4. _____

A. Where should we start?
B. What should we talk about today?
C. How would you like to use this time?
D. Would you like to begin with what you said last week?

5) Which of the following assessment instruments is rated by an outside observer?

5. _____

A. Family Assessment Device (FAD)
B. Family Cohesion and Adaptability Evaluation Scale (FACES)
C. Beavers Timberlawn Rating Scale (B-T)
D. Family Assessment Measure (FAM)

6) Which of the following is a technique of behavior therapy?   6. _____

A.   Family sculpting
B.   Scripting
C.   Contingency contracting
D.   Enactment

7) When a therapist does not place clear boundaries on the length   7. _____
of a session, one of the worst possible results in terms of treatment is that

A.   clients will feel that the therapist is not really paying attention
B.   client resistance to dealing with significant material promptly is reinforced
C.   client tardiness will increase
D.   clients will feel that their problems have taken on a greater importance

8) In the integration stage of therapy in human validation process   8. _____
model, the therapist

A.   assesses the level of family closeness
B.   encourages the expression of emotions
C.   investigates the presenting problem
D.   recognizes the resolution of turmoil

9) What type of family coalition is represented in the diagram below?   9. _____

A.   Disengaged
B.   Skewed
C.   Schismatic
D.   Pseudodemocratic

10) During a first therapy session, the therapist notices that a client   10. _____
uses unusual phrasing in her speech. From the object relations perspective,
this could be evidence of

A.   irrational role assignment
B.   a derivative
C.   differentiation
D.   collusion

11) Which of the following marital assessment instruments is used   11. _____
only in evaluating videotaped interactions?

A.   Marital Interaction Coding System (MICS)
B.   Verbal Problem Checklist (VPC)
C.   Primary Communications Inventory (PCI)
D.   Couples Interaction Scoring System (CISS)

12) Which of the following procedures would most likely be included   12. _____
in the long-term intrapsychic reconstruction phase of a treatment program
in the object relations model?

I.   Deepening the holding environment
II.   Observing interactions and free associations for derivatives
III.   Leaving defenses intact
IV.   Reducing symptoms

A.   I and II
B.   II and III
C.   III and IV
D.   I, II, III and IV

13) A married couple presents with a conflict. After the first session,   13. _____
the therapist sends them home with the following list of questions, to be
discussed during the next session:

1.   What did you expect of marriage before you got married?
2.   What did you expect of marriage just after you were married?
3.   What do you expect of marriage now?

In this exercise, the therapist is taking a(n) _____ approach to   13. _____
the problem.

A.   strategic
B.   object relations
C.   cognitive
D.   behavioral

14) Which of the following is typically done by a therapist latest in the   14. _____
process of structural family therapy?

A.   Assessing the family structure
B.   Raising session intensity
C.   Giving directives that restructure the family system
D.   Creating objectives

15)   Which of the following behaviors is the clearest example of   15. _____
"self-summarization syndrome"?

A.   A child repeatedly doing exactly the opposite of what a parent requests.
B.   A child crossing her arms and refusing to respond whenever a parent makes a
request--no matter how reasonable the request appears.
C.   A wife repeatedly responding to accusations of controlling behavior in an apologetic
tone that attributes her behavior to a personal defect.
D.   A husband saying to his wife, "You never listen to me!" repeatedly throughout a
session, with increasing emotional intensity.

16)   According to Bowen, the child who is most involved in the family   16. _____
emotional process emerges with the lowest level of differentiation, and passes
problems on to succeeding generations. This is an example of Bowen's concept of

A.   object relations
B.   the multigenerational transmission process
C.   an undifferentiated family ego mass
D.   the cross-generational coalition

17)   The "circular" patterns of communication commonly observed   17. _____
between couples in therapy include each of the following, except

A.   attack and defense
B.   vulnerability and reluctance
C.   rejection and inclusion
D.   anger and withdrawal

18)   Bowen systems therapy identifies four specific relationship   18. _____
strategies by which spouses attempt to handle anxiety. Which of the
following is not one of them?

A.   Symptom manipulation
B.   Marital conflict
C.   Emotional distance
D.   Child dysfunction

19)   Once a married couple decides to undergo conflict resolution,   19. _____
the therapist's first task is to

A.   help them understand the importance of good communication skills
B.   normalize the conflict
C.   explore the nature and depth of their commitment to each other
D.   help them understand the meaning and function of anger in their relationship

20)   A therapist sometimes seeks to detect, through the analysis of   20. _____
personal reactions to session material, the latent meaning behind a client's
attitudes, behaviors, or feelings. This hidden meaning is known as a

A.   branch
B.   derivative
C.   linkage
D.   projection

21)   During a conjoint therapy session, the wife says, "Every night   21. _____
when I come home from work, I try to be affectionate with my husband."
The most appropriate response on the part of the therapist would be to

A.   praise the wife for her sensitivity and caring
B.   ask the husband why he doesn't reciprocate
C.   ask the wife to explain why she feels the need to be affectionate at this time every
day
D.   ask both clients how the husband responds to the wife's displays of affection

22)   In operant behavior therapy, the study of a particular behavior,   22. _____
what elicits it, and what reinforces it is known as

A.   functional analysis
B.   prescription
C.   structural analysis
D.   drawing

23)   When a client expresses feelings in absolutes (I am always . . .   23. _____
She has never. . .), it is often a sign that

A.   the client is expressing false feelings to mask some other problem
B.   the client has or will assign blame for these feelings to a spouse or family member
C.   the feelings have direct historical roots from the client's early experiences and
relationships
D.   the feelings are more intense than other feelings experiences by the client

24)   Each of the following is a technique associated with structural   24. _____
family therapy, except

A.   mimesis
B.   joining
C.   tracking
D.   the pretend technique

25)   A family is in therapy, in part to explore the daughter's propensity   25. _____
to shoplift. The mother believes the daughter shoplifts because the father
unconsciously urges her to rebel against her mother. This explanation can be
described as

A.   dyadic
B.   triadic
C.   projective
D.   monadic

26)   A major shortcoming associated with the use of "good faith"   26. _____
contracts in marital and family therapy is their

A.   limitation to quantifiable behaviors
B.   requirement that certain behaviors are contingent upon others
C.   inflexibility in accommodating spontaneous situations
D.   focus on extrinsic rewards

27) The assumptions of experiential family therapy include: 27. _____

      I.   The therapist values spontaneity and genuineness in interactions
      II.   Individual growth improves family functioning
      III.   The therapist focuses primarily on changing individual functioning
      IV.   Personal therapy is an important prerequisite for the therapist to begin practice

A.   I only
B.   I and II
C.   II, III and IV
D.   I, II, III and IV

28) Which of the following models of therapy sometimes makes use   28. _____
of ordeals to alter symptom expression?

A.   Externalization
B.   Strategic
C.   MRI
D.   Solution-focused

29) During a marital therapy session, a husband declares that he   29. _____
believes oral sex to be wrong, implying that there's something wrong
with his wife for suggesting it. The wife responds that it isn't wrong,
and that there's something wrong with him for not wanting it. This is an example of

A.   using polarizing language
B.   personalization
C.   self-editing
D.   distracting from a discussion

30) In the structural model, subsystems are defined by redundant   30. _____
patterns organized across three dimensions. Which of the following is not
one of these dimensions?

A.   Behavioral activity
B.   Proximity
C.   Relative constructiveness
D.   Time

31) Of the five stages involved in a strategic family treatment interview,   31. _____
which occurs first?

A.   The problem stage
B.   The interaction stage
C.   The goal-setting stage
D.   The social stage

32) The squeeze technique is   32. _____

A.   a method used, along with sensate focus, to treat vaginismus
B.   an element of the self-stimulation paradigm
C.   a sex therapy technique used in the treatment of premature ejaculation
D.   an element of Minuchin's view of how family members become marginalized

33)   During an in-session interaction, a young child says to her   33. _____
father, "I hate you!" Which of the following replies on the part of the
father would be classified as a "reaction" rather than a "response"?

A.   I don't hate you, but I'd like to talk about it.
B.   What do you hate about me?
C.   What do you mean by that?
D.   Right now I don't much care for you either.

34)   A behaviorally oriented family therapist would use each of the   34. _____
following to teach communication, parenting, or problem-solving skills, except

A.   interpretive feedback
B.   verbal instruction and modeling of informational content
C.   descriptive feedback
D.   in-session rehearsal

35)   According to Bowen, which of the following characteristics is most 35. _____
significant in determining which child in a family will be most susceptible to
triangulation?

A.   Whether the child is a boy or a girl
B.   Whether the child is emotionally differentiated
C.   Whether the child is the oldest or youngest
D.   Whether the child exhibits behavior problems

36)   During conjoint therapy, a woman becomes upset and begins   36. _____
crying uncontrollably when her husband tells her he doesn't want to make
love to her when she isn't in the mood. Earlier in the relationship, she had
requently acquiesced when she was not in the mood. Which of the following
is the most likely reason for her crying at his statement?

A.   An overwhelming feeling of relief
B.   An emotional distortion--a response to historical experiences with narcissistic men
C.   Embarrassment at having the topic addressed in the therapist's presence
D.   A cognitive distortion--she takes his statement as a form of rejection

37)   Which of the following terms is frequently used to represent the   37. _____
difference between how members of a family relate and what they talk about?

A.   Enaction/Reaction
B.   Role-playing
C.   Vector/Focus
D.   Process/content

38)   In most dysfunctional families, the family member most likely   38. _____
to become symptomatic first is the

A.   mother
B.   father
C.   oldest child
D.   youngest child

39)   In a typical course of behavioral family treatment, which of the   39. _____
following would probably occur after the initial sessions?

A.   Determining contingencies of targeted behavior
B.   Establishing goals
C.   Monitoring and evaluating skill change
D.   Behavioral observations

40)   During a behavioral treatment program for a sexual problem,   40. _____
which of the following would generally occur first?

A.   An extensive sexual history involving both parties
B.   A thorough medical examination
C.   Provision of information about physiological processes associated with sex and
how they are influenced by anxiety
D.   Assignment of specific sexual techniques or exercises

41)   Which of the following is not a component of adjustment   41. _____
associated with the Dyadic Adjustment Scale (DAS) developed by Spanier?

A.   Dyadic cohesion
B.   Affectional expression
C.   Dyadic consensus
D.   Dyadic conflict

42)   The belief that client utterances have covert meanings refers to   42. _____
the _____ aspect of therapy.

A.   symbolic
B.   arcane
C.   conspiratorial
D.   experiential

43)   A strategic therapist could be expected to delegate   43. _____
out-of-session tasks

        I.   with the use of reframing
        II.   indirectly
        III.   without explanation
        IV.   paradoxically

A.   I only
B.   II and III
C.   II, III and IV
D.   I, II, III and IV

44)   An alliance between or among family members that serves   44. _____
a specific function or purpose is referred to as a(n)

A.   transference
B.   coalition
C.   bloc
D.   adherence

45) According to Madanes, behavioral problems are the result of   45. _____

A.   the desire to repent
B.   the desire to dominate and control others
C.   neglect
D.   learned helplessness

46) A therapist seeks to gain a thorough systemic understanding of a   46. _____
client's avowed anger. The most appropriate question for the therapist
to ask would be

A.   What happened to make you angry?
B.   Were either of your parents angry in a similar way?
C.   When did you realize this anger?
D.   Who causes you to be so angry?

47) Of the following types of household, the one that would be <u>least</u>   47. _____
likely to produce a schizophrenic relapse would be one that is

A.   a staging ground for consistently positive and happy emotions
B.   visited often by friends and relatives
C.   unstructured
D.   not organized around the illness

48) According to Whitaker, the initial phase of family treatment is   48. _____
characterized by

A.   the attempt to alleviate the presenting problem or symptom
B.   the therapist's insistence that family members assume responsibility for their own
growth and life decisions
C.   the recognition of all relevant feelings that need to be honored in family interactions
D.   the family's struggle to control therapy

49) In structural family therapy, the selection of an area of family   49. _____
interaction for exploration is known as

A.   enactment
B.   mimesis
C.   focus
D.   winnowing

50) In order to begin a treatment program together, partners in a   50. _____
couple generally need to agree on

        I.   what the problem is
        II.   who most needs to change
        III. whether the presented problem is the real problem
        IV.   the desired resolution of the problem

A.   I only
B.   I and IV
C.   I, II and III
D.   I, II, III and IV

KEY (CORRECT ANSWERS)

1.	D		41.	D
2.	A		42.	A
3.	B		43.	D
4.	D		44.	B
5.	C		45.	B
6.	C		46.	B
7.	B		47.	D
8.	D		48.	D
9.	B		49.	C
10.	B		50.	B
11.	D			
12.	A			
13.	C			
14.	D			
15.	D			
16.	B			
17.	C			
18.	A			
19.	B			
20.	B			
21.	D			
22.	A			
23.	C			
24.	D			
25.	B			
26.	D			
27.	D			
28.	B			
29.	A			
30.	C			
31.	D			
32.	C			
33.	D			
34.	A			
35.	C			
36.	B			
37.	D			
38.	A			
39.	C			
40.	B			

TEST 3

Directions: Each question or incomplete statement is followed by several suggested answers or completions. Select the one the BEST answers the question or completes the statement. *PRINT THE LETTER OF THE CORRECT ANSWER IN THE SPACE AT THE RIGHT.*

1)   Which of the following statements about systemic family   1. _____
therapy is <u>true</u>?

A.   It involves only the family members who report a problem
B.   Its interventions are delivered as opinions or requests for extrasession behavior
changes
C.   It focuses on only dysfunctional behaviors
D.   It uses specific behavioral goals to bring about change

2)   When a therapist wants to stimulate quantum leaps in a client's   2. _____
behavior, he/she is most likely to assign _____ tasks.

A.   In-session
B.   Paradoxical
C.   Repetitive
D.   Linear

3)   The diagram below is associated with the _____   3. _____
model
of family therapy.

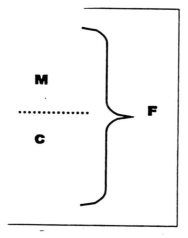

A.   object relations
B.   structural
C.   Bowen systems
D.   strategic

4)   During a heated discussion between a married couple, a therapist   4. _____
interrupts the wife and says, "Can you see what you were doing just now?"
The wife responds, "I was stating my opinion." The therapist says, "You were
stating it in a very judgemental way." Here, the therapist is

A.   role-playing
B.   exposing the presenting problem
C.   initiating an enactment
D.   forming an implicit coalition with the husband

5)   Of the following, which is usually initiated by a therapist latest   5. _____
in the process of conflict resolution?

A.   Normalizing the conflict
B.   Assessing the meaning of anger in the relationship
C.   Bibliotherapy
D.   A lesson in fair fighting

6)   A therapist has spent the last several months in sessions with   6. _____
a married couple, whom the therapist believes to have presented a unique
and instructive problem. The therapist would like to publish an article about
their case, in order to inform other therapists. During a one-on-one session
with the wife, the therapist explains his wish and asks the wife if she will sign
a waiver of confidentiality that will allow the therapist to disclose the content of
their previous joint sessions. The wife agrees, and signs the waiver. Which of the
following is true?

A.   The therapist is free to disclose anything that transpired during their sessions.
B.   The therapist may only disclose words that were spoken by or about the wife.
C.   The therapist may only disclose information to prevent a clear and immediate danger
to someone
D.   The therapist cannot reveal anything of the sessions until the husband has also
signed the waiver.

7)   During therapy with a married couple, a wife reports several threats 7. _____
of physical violence made by the husband. Both husband and wife insist that
none of the threats have been carried out. The therapists responds by telling
the husband, "You're all talk. When are you going to be man enough to follow
through?" This therapist is working in the _____ model.

A.   experiential
B.   object relations
C.   integrated
D.   contextual

8)   Which of the following assessment instruments is reported by an   8. _____
external observer of the married couple?

A.   Marital Observation Checklist (MOC)
B.   Marital Adjustment Scale (MAS)
C.   Couples Interaction Scoring System (CISS)
D.   Primary Communication Inventory (PCI)

9)   Which of the following is a concept used in structural   9. _____
family therapy?

A.   Subsystem
B.   Circular causality
C.   Triangulation
D.   Boundary

10)   Integrative family therapy comprises a blend of each of the   10. _____
following approaches, <u>except</u>

A.   structural
B.   strategic
C.   experiential
D.   behavioral

11)   Between married couples in the 22-28 age group who experience   11. _____
marital conflict, the conflict is most likely to have its roots in

A.   differing ways of achieving productivity
B.   uncertainty about the choice of partner
C.   conflicting rates and directions of emotional growth
D.   conflicting ties to the family of origin

12)   In general, most strategic tasks are designed to manipulate   12. _____

A.   only the person with the symptom
B.   the entire family
C.   the person least invested in changing
D.   the symptom

13)   Which of the following would be most appropriately verbalized   13. _____
by a therapist during the early assessment sessions of therapy?

A.   The goals of therapy
B.   A summary of each spouse/family member's concerns
C.   The "ground rules" of treatment
D.   Feedback regarding marital/family strengths/weaknesses

14)   Which of the following models of family therapy tends to   14. _____
reject theory to the greatest degree?

A.   Experiential
B.   Contextual
C.   Bowenian
D.   Communications (MRI)

15)   The structural elements of out-of-session "homework" assigned   15. _____
by the therapist are

A.   conception, execution, result
B.   cognition, behavior, affect
C.   time, duration, frequency, place
D.   self, marriage, spouse, children

16) During a session with a family, it is revealed that the couple's   16. _____
young son wakes up every night and is brought into the couple's bed.
This is probably an issue that should be approached

A.   structurally
B.   contextually
C.   behaviorally
D.   experientially

17) During the evaluation phase of conjoint treatment, the level of   17. _____
emotional intensity between the two partners is observed to escalate by
the therapist. The therapist will probably continue this escalation if he/she
asks a question that begins with

A.   Who
B.   When
C.   Why
D.   What

18) A therapist is preparing a schematic genogram of a family system.   18. _____
Which of the following symbols is typically used to represent children?

A.   Horizontal line
B.   Square
C.   Vertical line
D.   Circle

19) Typically, a therapist implementing a symbolic-experiential   19. _____
treatment program will begin the first stage of treatment in a role that can
best be compared to

A.   the age mate of a young child
B.   an older, competitive sibling
C.   the dominant parent of a young child
D.   the retired parent of an adult child

20) Of the following models of family therapy, which is/are   20. _____
concerned with the influence of family hierarchy on the development
of symptoms?

I.   Strategic
II.   Structural
III.   Solution-focused
IV.   MRI

A.   I and II
B.   II and III
C.   III and IV
D.   None of the above

21) The primary objective of Bowen systems therapy is best described as

    21. _____

A. heightening the individual's emotional experience
B. translating intraindividual gains into more functional responses
C. lessen the distress associated with the presenting problem
D. helping clients achieve a higher level of self-differentiation

22) A family in treatment is characterized by an overemphasis on the children. This family would probably be typed as

    22. _____

A. internalized
B. constricted
C. object-focused
D. chaotic

23) In the Milan approach to family therapy, a specific act is sometimes prescribed for a family to perform that will change the family system's rules. The act is typically referred to as

    23. _____

A. a ritual
B. a script
C. a myth
D. an enactment

24) A therapist wants to describe the concept of negative entitlement for a couple, but wants to avoid professional jargon. She decides upon the use of an analogy. Which of the following is most suitable?

    24. _____

A. Not letting new information cloud decisions of the past.
B. A green light.
C. Being unable to complete the final paper of the final class required for a degree.
D. A party invitation that doesn't name a time or date

25) Gestalt-experiential family therapy views psychological problems as the result of

    25. _____

A. a faulty perspective
B. incomplete encounters
C. emotional regression
D. a failure to attach

26) Each of the following models of family therapy makes use of metaphor, except

    26. _____

A. human validation process
B. MRI
C. structural
D. strategic

27) Which of the following statements is generally supported by   27. _____
research in marital communication?

A.   Distressed spouses do not perceive their partners' communications more negatively than nondistressed couples.
B.   There are no major differences between the quality of the casual conversations of distressed and nondistressed couples.
C.   Distressed couples exhibit a greater disagreement to agreement ratio
D.   Distressed and nondistressed couples generally differ with respect to the intention of their communications.

28) Which of the following elements of marital contracting is most   28. _____
at risk for underemphasis by a therapist?

A.   Avoiding the use of punishment
B.   Monitoring progress
C.   Inclusiveness
D.   Realistic expectations

29) According to Whitaker, which of the following is/are true when   29. _____
both a "white knight" and a "black sheep" exist in a family?

    I.   The apparent mental health advantage of the white knight over the black sheep is illusory
    II.   The black sheep sacrifices him/herself to help the family achieve success
    III.   Both are victims of the larger family system.
    IV.   One's role is always assumed in opposition to the other

A.   I only
B.   I and III
C.   II, III and IV
D.   I, II, III and IV

30) A couple presents to a therapist with difficulty in becoming more   30. _____
intimate, although they have some awareness of what it means and what
they want. In the initial stage of addressing this problem, the therapist would
probably keep the discussion framed in terms of

A.   competition
B.   love
C.   giving
D.   fear

31) The "next-step" mentality sometimes adopted by families in   31. _____
therapy is the assumption that

A.   problems are always consequences in themselves
B.   the problem is one of symbolism
C.   tasks should not literally conform to the problem
D.   an intervention should be a logical response to a problem

32)	A family reports to therapy with their 14-year-old daughter,	32. _____
Julia, as the identified patient. Julia's older brother and her mother and
father describe her as being rebellious. A good first step for the therapist
would be to

A.	structure an enactment
B.	request a few minutes alone with Julia, in order to focus on her and orient treatment
to her problem
C.	ask each member to define what he/she means by "rebellious"
D.	ask Julia to respond to these accusations

33)	According to Minuchin, maladaptive family transactions may be	33. _____
changed by means of each of the following, <u>except</u>

A.	strong affect
B.	deep enmeshment
C.	prolonged pressure
D.	repeated intervention

34)	When asked to explain his tendency to lose his temper, a son says	34. _____
to his mother, "I can't help it--when you talk to me like that, I can't control
what I'm doing. You should know that and stop talking to me like that." Of
the four methods of destructive linear attribution identified by Strong and Claiborn, the son
is practicing

A.	debilitation
B.	justification
C.	rationalization
D.	vilification

35)	Solution-focused therapy assumes that the presence of an ongoing	35. _____
problem in a family creates

A.	expanding behavioral sequences
B.	a fixation of roles
C.	ordeals
D.	a narrowing of perspective

36)	The idea that marital problems occur when spouses have	36. _____
unrealistic expectations of each other, and then make extreme self-statements
on the basis of these expectations, is the foundation of _____ therapy.

A.	self-referential
B.	cognitive
C.	ideocentric
D.	rational-emotive

37) A structural therapist, working with a family which includes   37. _____
an anorexic client, would be most likely to

A. have the family switch chairs, so that each may experience a deficient holding environment
B. ask the anorexic to identify parts of herself that are associated with early trauma
C. have the family attend a lunchtime session, in order to observer patterns associated with eating
D. have the family bring the grandparents to therapy, in order to increase spontaneity

38) According to structural theory, behavior problems are usually   38. _____
the result of

A. a strict hierarchy between the spousal and parental subsystems
B. historical patterns derived from each parent's family of origin
C. insufficient conditioning
D. a nonhierarchical arrangement of parent and child subsystems

39) In the systems model, the major strategy in reducing family   39. _____
resistance to therapy is

A. strategic interventions
B. behavioral interventions
C. interpretations
D. bibliotherapy

40) Which of the following is usually involved in nearly all forms   40. _____
of treatment for sexual dysfunction?

A. Medication
B. Desensitization
C. Role-playing
D. Dilators

41) During an intake interview, a couple expresses a desire to remedy   41. _____
growing dissatisfaction in their marriage. It is revealed later in the session
that the husband is carrying on a relationship with a woman at his workplace,
of which the wife is aware. The husband speaks dismissively of the relationship
as "no big deal," and the wife says she isn't sure what's happened between them
in the past--and she's not sure what's happening now. Which of the following
actions is probably most appropriate for the therapist to take in this situation?

A. Ask the husband directly whether the relationship is sexual.
B. Ask questions that will lead to an understanding of the wife's denial of the affair's seriousness.
C. Ask leading questions to get the husband to reveal voluntarily whether the relationship is sexual.
D. Express a warm desire to help the couple, but insist that therapy can't begin unless the relationship with the woman is terminated entirely.

42) According to Satir, family members often demonstrate one of five   42. _____
universal patterns of interaction. Of these, which is characterized as "outwardly
immobile, inwardly vulnerable"?

A.   Leveller
B.   Distractor
C.   Placator
D.   Computer

43) Which of the following marital assessment instruments is the   43. _____
most widely used for the direct observation and analysis of couples' interactions?

A.   Marital Interaction Coding System (MICS)
B.   Verbal Problem Checklist (VPC)
C.   Primary Communications Inventory (PCI)
D.   Couples Interaction Scoring System (CISS)

44) In most traditional families, the husband's role is described as   44. _____

A.   expressive
B.   prescriptive
C.   instrumental
D.   transferent

45) The Bowenian genogram below denotes   45. _____

A.   the birth of a girl
B.   the abortion of boy
C.   the adoption of a girl
D.   the conception of a girl

46) Which of the following is an assumption associated with   46. _____
systemic family therapy?

A.   The interventions are aimed at one family member at a time.
B.   Symptoms in the system do not serve any specific function.
C.   Symptoms are alleviated because of an altering of hierarchies.
D.   If a single component in the family system changes, the entire system must change.

47) Of the following treatment types or settings, which generally 47. _____
involves the lowest improvement rate in nonbehavioral marital and family
therapy?

A. Individual
B. Conjoint
C. Conjoint group
D. Concurrent

48) Which of the following is a covert means by which a family 48. _____
therapist can manipulate a family structure?

A. Raising intensity
B. Challenging attributional sets
C. Commenting on and altering the process
D. Using enactments

49) When first dealing with a couple that includes an alcoholic 49. _____
partner, the therapist should most likely adopt a role like that of a

A. facilitator discussion
B. teacher or expert consultant
C. passive observer
D. close friend

50) According to the behavioral model, aggressive and coercive child 50. _____
behavior

A. begins in the family
B. is a response to trauma
C. can be channeled into constructive pursuits
D. is extinguished by peers

KEY (CORRECT ANSWERS)

1. B	41. D
2. B	42. D
3. B	43. A
4. D	44. C
5. D	45. C
6. D	46. D
7. A	47. A
8. C	48. B
9. D	49. B
10. B	50. A
11. B	
12. D	
13. B	
14. A	
15. C	
16. C	
17. C	
18. C	
19. C	
20. A	
21. D	
22. C	
23. A	
24. C	
25. B	
26. C	
27. B	
28. B	
29. B	
30. D	
31. D	
32. C	
33. B	
34. A	
35. D	
36. D	
37. C	
38. D	
39. A	
40. B	

EXAMINATION SECTION

DIRECTIONS: Each question or incomplete statement is followed by several suggested answers or completions. Select the one that BEST answers the question or completes the statement. *PRINT THE LETTER OF THE CORRECT ANSWER IN THE SPACE AT THE RIGHT.*

1. Which of the following mechanisms function to reinforce impulse control?   1._____
    - I.   Projection
    - II. Diverting attention to other areas
    - III. Fantasy
    - IV. Identification
    - V.   Furtherance of another impulse demand less dangerous than the original

    The CORRECT answer is:
    - A. I, II, IV
    - B. II, III, IV, V
    - C. II, V
    - D. II, III, IV
    - E. All of the above

2. Which of the following are intervention guides?   2._____
    - I.   Themes that indicate matters of concern to the patient
    - II. Areas of omission
    - III. Contradictions
    - IV. Response to stimuli
    - V.   Vagueness and confusion

    The CORRECT answer is:
    - A. I, III, IV
    - B. I, II
    - C. I, IV, V
    - D. All of the above
    - E. None of the above

3. Proper timing in investigative therapy involves   3._____
    - I.   motivation
    - II. eliminating anxiety
    - III. involvement
    - IV. mutual understanding of the message issue
    - V.   limiting investment

    The CORRECT answer is:
    - A. I, II, III
    - B. I, II, IV
    - C. I, III, IV
    - D. I, II, III, IV
    - E. All of the above

4. Which of the following are used to reduce anxiety to effect learning?   4._____
    - I.   Fortuitive subject changes
    - II. Clarifying the problem
    - III. Maintaining focus on a specific issue
    - IV. Support
    - V.   Concrete rather than abstract communication

    The CORRECT answer is:
    - A. I, II, III
    - B. I, III, IV
    - C. II, III, IV, V
    - D. I, IV, V
    - E. All of the above

5. Which of the following are true of transference?   5._____
   I.   It is most frequently based on parental figures
   II. It usually remains constant
   III. Elements of transference usually develop in a long-term
        relationship with a patient
   IV. Transference is usually a phenomenon reserved solely for the
        therapist working with the patient
   V.   The original figures upon whom present distortions are based
        may remain constant or may alternate

   The CORRECT answer is:
   A. I, II, III   B. I, III, IV   C. I, II, III, IV   D. I, III, V
   E. All of the above

6. The dyadic relationship as a valuable treatment modality in psychiatry has   6._____
   been conceptualized in all of the following ways EXCEPT to
   A. *provide* recreational diversion
   B. *offer* guidance and advice
   C. *further* the patient's dependence on the relationship
   D. *expand* the patient's exploration of problematic thoughts
   E. *encourage* socially appropriate grooming and habits

7. The therapist assists the patient in a dyadic relationship in all of the   7._____
   following ways EXCEPT helping the patient to
   A. *review* his experiences
   B. *create* an anxiety-free environment
   C. *clarify* his distortions
   D. *understand* his participation in creating and maintaining
      troublesome experiences
   E. *derive* new meanings from his experiences

8. According to Freud, anxiety is the product of   8._____
   A. impulse   B. stimulation   C. inhibition   D. conflict
   E. projection

9. In which areas should verbal intervention be effected?   9._____
   A. In those areas only in which the therapist can be effective
   B. Only in the areas of minimal resistance
   C. Only in the areas that do not produce stress
   D. The most problematic areas
   E. In all areas

10. Distortions and misperceptions caused by transference are reduced by all   10._____
    of the following EXCEPT:
    A. Contacts between therapist and patient are varied
    B. Contacts between therapist and patient are made less available
    C. Spontaneity is reduced but not eliminated
    D. Less-structured interactions are encouraged
    E. Contacts between therapist and patient are characterized by
       freedom to express oneself as a "real" person and not in a role

2

11. The task of supporting and reinforcing the patient's independence and assertiveness occurs
    A. *when* the dyadic relationship is being formed
    B. *prior* to the onset of termination
    C. *during* the initial stages of termination
    D. *during* the concluding stages of termination
    E. *after* the termination process has been completed

    11._____

12. Which phase of Group Therapy is the stage of GREATEST equilibrium in which consensus is easily reached and socially deviant behavior is at a minimum?
    A. Getting-acquainted stage
    B. Minor acting-out phase
    C. Major acting-out phase
    D. The stage when the group becomes a group
    E. Termination of the group stage

    12._____

13. What information for a Situation Analysis Model approach to the study of psychotherapy groups is included in the area of "setting?" The
    A. nature of the institution and the characteristics of the clientele
    B. emerging interactional patterns among the group members
    C. nature of the conflict as related to the focal event
    D. physical location and intervening aspects of the room
    E. background information that seems significantly related to the focal point

    13._____

14. The treatment approach to family therapy involves
    A. hospitalization of the family member who exhibited the most apparent psychopathologic symptoms
    B. hospitalization of the family member identified as the catalyst
    C. hospitalization of key family members
    D. hospitalization of any family members maintaining dysfunctional relationships
    E. outpatient therapy that rarely necessitates hospitalization of any family member

    14._____

15. Occupational and recreational therapies employed during the course of family therapy provide valuable opportunities for
    A. acting-out behavior
    B. release of aggression
    C. improving dissatisfaction with unit policies
    D. establishing independence from the family
    E. individual accomplishment

    15._____

16. What is the crux of nursing practice on the Family Therapy Unit?　　　　16._____
    A. Developing in the patient an ability to examine his own behavior and how it affects the responses of others
    B. Assisting patients to understand themselves through the relationships they establish with other persons
    C. To increase the patient's understanding of verbal and non-verbal communications
    D. To help the patient acquire an appreciation of the problems and feelings of his family
    E. Assisting the patient to understand the underlying goals of staff intervention and how these affect the treatment process

17. All of the following are *disadvantages* in using co-therapists in Family　　　　17._____
    Therapy EXCEPT:
    A. Feelings of competitiveness arise between the therapists
    B. There is disagreement in their approach to treatment
    C. Lack of mutual respect often results
    D. One of the co-therapists dominates
    E. One co-therapist may support one member of the family while the other co-therapist simultaneously supports another during the conferences

18. Which of the following is considered the PRIME goal of modern　　　　18._____
    psychiatry?
    A. Improving diagnostic methods
    B. Improving therapeutic methods
    C. Focusing on intrafamilial problems
    D. Educating and training interdisciplinary staff members
    E. Emphasizing preventative psychiatry

19. Which of the following is the BEST definition of grief? It is a response to　　　　19._____
    the loss
    A. through death or separation of a loved person
    B. of a position of status
    C. of a prized faculty
    D. of self-esteem, a cherished self-image or a loved one
    E. the loss of anything tangible or intangible which is highly valued

20. Which of the following questions BEST describes utilization of the dyadic　　　　20._____
    relationship?
    A. How can nurses use the relationship most effectively in terms of time and effort?
    B. How should non-professionals' use of the relationship be considered?
    C. What universal view of the therapeutic use of the relationship can be adopted?
    D. How does the nurse delineate professional and non-professional roles?
    E. What skills are required for use of this relationship?

21. Which of the following BEST describes the progress most patients make toward awareness of their participation in, and their distortion of, events during dyadic relationship therapy?
    A. Total lack of improvement
    B. Total awareness preceded by little or no progress
    C. Minute and fleeting indications of improvement
    D. Quick, steady progress
    E. Slow, steady progress

21._____

22. Most frequently, the ego's defense against an id impulse implies that the impulse is deemed threatening because of
    A. ethical values
    B. social values
    C. internal prohibitions that relate to present reality factors
    D. internal prohibitions that relate to prior conflictual experiences
    E. internal prohibitions that relate to external factors

22._____

23. How does Ruesch define "Feedback?" A means of
    A. re-evaluating past action by an organism
    B. reducing distortion
    C. determining the worth of ongoing action
    D. transfer of information
    E. returning information about ongoing action to the organism

23._____

24. Which of the following is NOT a valid reason to deal with the patient's perception of his position prior to dealing with the nurse's perception of it? It enables
    A. the nurse to determine where her initial efforts should be directed
    B. the nurse to see how the patient views significant experiences and persons in his life
    C. the nurse to determine how the patient protects himself from unpleasant internal or external realities
    D. the nurse to alter the patient's motivation
    E. the establishment of a relationship between nurse and patient

24._____

25. Distortion, repetition and lack of complementarity are characteristics of
    A. anxiety   B. separation
    C. conflict   D. transference
    E. counter-transference

25._____

26. Which of the following BEST describes what the patient feels at the onset of termination of the dyadic relationship? The patient feels
    A. a loss of identity   B. a lack of control
    C. acute turmoil   D. guilty
    E. relief

26._____

27. Which phase of Group Therapy is the *major* acting-out phase?
    A. Orientation   B. Minor acting-out
    C. Crescendo of tension   D. Termination of the group
    E. "When the group becomes a group"

27._____

28. All of the following information is included in the area of "situation" for a   28._____
    Situation Analysis Model approach to the study of psychotherapy groups
    EXCEPT the
    A. precipitating event
    B. focal event
    C. pertinent individual psychodynamics
    D. therapist's intervention
    E. effects and implications of the group experience

29. Family Therapy is aimed at   29._____
    A. reducing the levels of anxiety
    B. having family members view the primary patient in a more realistic
       way
    C. assessing the kinds of problems family members have in relating
       and communicating to one another
    D. having family members understand their destructive and often
       painful relationships are due to symptoms seen in the primary
       patient
    E. integrating the primary patient back into the family unit

30. Which of the following is a fairly reliable indication of the family's   30._____
    motivation to go through Family Therapy successfully?
    A. Willingness to commit themselves to treatment
    B. Realization that their relationships are unuseful or dysfunctional
    C. Attendance at the weekly family conferences
    D. Attendance at the weekly relatives' group meetings
    E. Setting realistic goals for themselves and the hospitalized member

31. What characterizes Family Therapy's primary patient's initial attempts to   31._____
    define his relationships with staff and other patients?
    A. Acting and relating in a manner similar to his interaction with the
       family
    B. Acting in a way he perceives will be viewed as healthy
    C. Rejection and hostility toward staff and other patients
    D. Acting and relating in a manner that indicates his need for
       acceptance
    E. Acting and relating in a way the therapeutic milieu suggests he
       should

32. Families do *not* become really engaged in treatment UNTIL   32._____
    A. their initial resistive defensiveness is worked through
    B. they're willing to commit themselves to treatment
    C. they're released from inhibitions concerned with identification and
       expression of wishes and goals
    D. they become involved in both the family conferences and the
       relatives' group meetings
    E. family members stop family members from employing incongruent
       and double-message communication techniques

6

33. What is *primary* prevention of mental health disorders? Lowering the rate
    of new cases by
    A. counteracting harmful circumstances before they have produced
       illness
    B. screening children through the school system
    C. improving the social environment
    D. helping non-psychiatric physicians utilize psychoanalytic concepts
    E. expanding the mental health program to educate citizens and
       establish community residences for hospitalized patients

33._____

34. What is the CHIEF developmental task during infancy?
    A. Initiation of the process of differentiation from the mother
    B. Establishment of ego identity through the process of separation
       and the accompanying mourning
    C. Implementation of the infant ego through maternal care
    D. Winning recognition through the process of mastery
    E. Development of self-control and self-esteem

34._____

35. The investigative approach involved in exploratory therapy is directed
    toward
    A. understanding the patient's feelings
    B. focusing attention on certain aspects of the patient's experience
       and facilitating the patient's scrutiny of his actions
    C. supportive therapy
    D. focusing on external support and structure
    E. modes relying upon activities to convey a message

35._____

36. What is the result when the patient begins to be aware of his participation
    in and distortion of events?
    A. A sense of hopelessness and helplessness
    B. Increased anxiety and/or guilt
    C. Withdrawal
    D. Hostility
    E. A sense of well-being

36._____

37. Anxiety reduction occurs when the ego
    A. initiates means of inhibiting id impulse expression
    B. does not offer resistance to id impulse expression
    C. does not allow internal or external stimulation of an id impulse
    D. accepts the id impulse
    E. complements the id

37._____

38. What is the objective of communication in investigative therapy?
    A. Assessing the kinds and extents of problems that the patient has
    B. Effective problem-solving skills
    C. Behavioral alteration through understanding
    D. Establishment of external support and structure
    E. Prevention of therapeutic despair

38._____

39. What factor contributes the structure essential to mutual understanding
    and the work of therapy?
    A. Timing   B. Environment
    C. Clinical sensitivity   D. Communication
    E. Clarity

39._____

40. The development of transference is MOST influenced by the   40._____
      A. amount and type of contact
      B. degree of spontaneity
      C. environment
      D. patient's current relationships with others
      E. therapist

41. When the termination phase of a dyadic relationship has been completed,   41._____
contact between the patient and the therapist *should*
      A. gradually, over a period of time, diminish
      B. continue as long as the patient desires it
      C. continue on an intermittent basis
      D. continue until the patient is fully integrated on the outside
      E. terminate

42. Which phase of Group Therapy is the stage when pairing, complaining   42._____
and regression are observed among the participants?
      A. Orientation   B. Minor acting-out
      C. Major acting-out   D. Termination of the group
      E. "When the group becomes a group"

43. A Situation Analysis Model approach to the study of psychotherapy   43._____
groups calls the specific occurrence that catalyzes the group reaction
      A. the focal event   B. therapist intervention
      C. therapist interaction   D. group dynamics
      E. the precipitating event

44. What is the area of Family Therapy concentration?   44._____
      A. Authority   B. Communication
      C. Goals   D. Anxiety
      E. Environment

45. What is the CHIEF benefit of Family Therapy's Relatives' Group   45._____
Meetings?
      A. It creates a bond that facilitates expression and exchange of
            feelings
      B. It allows relatives to exchange experiences and set realistic goals
            for themselves
      C. The bonding that occurs facilitates the learning of basic group
            problem-solving skills
      D. The support of the group allows expression of dissatisfaction with
            current unit policies
      E. The sharing that occurs helps families deal with the hospitalized
            member in a more realistic way

46. Which of the following is the *most limiting* aspect of the use of psychiatric   46._____
aides? Their
      A. educational background
      B. own self-perceptions of their worth and value
      C. ability
      D. excessive verbal participation on the team
      E. inability to observe or understand their interaction with patients

47. Family members most often employ incongruent and double-message communication techniques as a result of
    A. being forced to assume responsibility for their actions
    B. distortions of reality
    C. a combination of their need to be understood and their fear of what may happen if they are really understood
    D. inability to separate assumptions and impressions from fact
    E. an unconscious desire to maintain the status quo even when it is apparent that the primary patient is getting better

47._____

48. Which of the following is considered the *most appropriate* area of which to focus attention in the primary prevention of mental health disorders?
    A. Improvement of unsound housing
    B. Increasing the resistance of the individual
    C. Improving poor living conditions
    D. Educating the public
    E. Establishment of community centers

48._____

49. During the infancy stage of development, the early phase of unrelatedness and transference is replaced by
    A. the process of individuation
    B. differentiation
    C. an autistic stage
    D. a sense of symbiotic fusion
    E. the phase of separation

49._____

50. Which of the following is an *inherent* aspect of any psychiatric treatment form?
    A. Self understanding
    B. Verbal interaction
    C. Activities to convey a message
    D. Anxiety relief
    E. Supportive measures

50._____

KEY (CORRECT ANSWERS)

1. E	11. D	21. C	31. A	41. E
2. D	12. A	22. D	32. A	42. B
3. C	13. E	23. E	33. A	43. E
4. D	14. A	24. D	34. A	44. B
5. D	15. E	25. D	35. B	45. A
6. C	16. B	26. B	36. B	46. B
7. B	17. E	27. C	37. A	47. C
8. D	18. E	28. C	38. C	48. B
9. A	19. E	29. C	39. E	49. D
10. B	20. A	30. D	40. A	50. E

EXAMINATION SECTION

DIRECTIONS: Each question or incomplete statement is followed by several suggested answers or completions. Select the one that BEST answers the question or completes the statement. PRINT THE LETTER OF THE CORRECT ANSWER IN THE SPACE AT THE RIGHT.

1. *Which* of the following are used to increase anxiety   1.___
   and mobilize the patient to effect learning?
     I. Support
    II. Clarifying the problem
   III. Deterring invasion
    IV. Maintaining focus on specific issues
     V. Using concrete rather than abstract communication
   The CORRECT answer is:
     A. I, II, III   B. I, III, IV, V   C. II, III, IV
     D. II, III, IV, V   E. All of the above

2. *Which* of the following phases of the dyadic relation-   2.___
   ship are vital to what is to follow?
     I. Initiating the relationship
    II. Interviewing
   III. Clarification and validation
    IV. Working through
     V. Termination
   The CORRECT answer is:
     A. I, III   B. II, IV   C. I, V
     D. III, IV   E. IV, V

3. In order to justify intervention in regressive behavior,   3.___
   which of the following *must* be present?
     I. There must be behavior in progress that is defined
        in a given social system as regressive
    II. There must have been behavior on a higher develop-
        mental level prior to the regressive behavior
   III. There must be a general consensus that a patient
        has regressed and that intervention is a necessary
        step
    IV. Intervention must be based on the proposition
        that it is necessary for the patient to progress
        to a higher level
     V. Regressive behavior brings out varied feelings
        in both staff and patients, and the patient may
        try to overcome or deny the process of regression
   The CORRECT answer is:
     A. I, II, III, IV B. I, IV, V   C. I, III
     D. I, III, IV   E. All of the above

4. *Which* of the following are TRUE of families when they   4.___
   are first encountered in Family Unit Treatment Centers?
   They
      I. are afraid to be blamed for the primary patient's
         illness
     II. rarely see themselves as having problems
    III. seldom realize the effect of their own behavior
         and problems on the primary patient
     IV. often use the treatment situation to express their
         disagreements with each other
      V. compete with each other, trying to manipulate
         the therapists to choose one member's side over
         another
   The CORRECT answer is:
      A. I, III, V   B. I, II, III   C. I, II, V
      D. I, III, IV   E. All of the above

5. *Which* of the following factors are related to a higher   5.___
   incidence of mental disorder?
      I. Overcrowding
     II. Low socioeconomic status
    III. Insufficient food
     IV. Lack of relationships within the community
      V. Unemployment
   The CORRECT answer is:
      A. I, IV, V   B. I, II, V   C. I, IV
      D. I, II, IV, V   E. All of the above

6. A patient experiencing acute turmoil and disintegration   6.___
   requires an approach that *primarily* stresses
      A. attention on certain aspects of the patient's
         experience
      B. patient functioning and self-understanding
      C. verbal interaction and identification of feelings,
         thoughts, and actions
      D. external support and provision of an identification
         figure
      E. activities used to convey a message

7. When using a dyadic relationship as a therapeutic vehicle,   7.___
   therapeutic despair *frequently* is the result of
      A. lack of patient improvement
      B. therapist anxiety
      C. patient guilt
      D. the therapist's identification with the patient
      E. the unpleasant thoughts and feelings engendered
         by the patient during the therapeutic process

8. All of the following are *true* of defense mechanisms   8.___
   used to control conflict EXCEPT: They
      A. inhibit healthy functioning
      B. are not always effective
      C. may allow maladaptive patterns to develop
      D. may reduce the ego's adaptive capacity
      E. are part of every person's adaptive capacity

9. Relevant information and a desire to alter behavior   9.___
   are not sufficient to effect change for
       A. long-standing modes of interaction
       B. problematic behavior
       C. behavior based on social courtesies
       D. benign failure to force attention on particular
          behavior
       E. behavioral adaptation to conflict

10. *What* is the effect of a double-bind message? It
       A. *prohibits* intervention
       B. *may lead to* doubt and confusion
       C. *causes* reduction of intense anxiety
       D. *results in* clinical sensitivity and goal maintenance
       E. *focuses on* overcoming resistance and altering awareness

11. *Which* of the following is the *least likely* explanation   11.___
    of why transference occurs? It
       A. is an attempt to master traumatic situations
       B. is a reaction to new stimuli that require new
          responses
       C. is the product of conflict
       D. encourages others to respond in a complementary
          role
       E. is a way of avoiding threatening issues

12. All of the following are essential to terminating therapy 12.___
    EXCEPT:
       A. Disappearance of symptoms
       B. Development of the ability to cope effectively
          with difficulties
       C. Disappearance of patient distortions
       D. Self-understanding
       E. Self-realization

13. *Which* phase of Group Therapy is the stage in which   13.___
    the main purpose appears to be testing the limits of
    the situation?
       A. Getting-acquainted stage
       B. Minor acting-out phase
       C. Major acting-out phase
       D. The stage when the group becomes a group
       E. Termination of the group stage

14. A Situation Analysis Model approach to the study of   14.___
    psychotherapy groups details data to be used for analysis.
    Therapist intervention appears to be crucial when she
    responds to the groups' reaction to
       A. the setting
       B. the precipitating event
       C. individual psychodynamics
       D. the focal event
       E. her intervention

15. *Why* is each member of the family given a screening   15.____
    interview prior to family therapy treatment? To
    A. determine the nature of the problem
    B. construct a program of therapy
    C. collect data relevant to the treatment of the
       primary patient
    D. determine which members should be hospitalized
    E. determine whether the problem can be treated and
       whether the family is willing to commit its members
       to treatment

16. *What* is the *principal purpose* of the inclusion of a   16.____
    nurse as an active participant in the Family Therapy
    phase of the relatives' group meeting? To
    A. provide a beginning group experience from which
       the nursing staff member can enhance the quality
       of her functioning as a psychiatric nurse
    B. increase recognition of difficult skills and talents
       delineated along disciplinary lines
    C. provide the staff with a Situation Analysis Model
    D. evaluate the treatment process of the ongoing
       group
    E. provide additional support to the relatives of
       the primary patient

17. *What* is the nurse's task in dealing with the newly   17.____
    admitted primary patient of a Family Therapy Group?
    A. Identifying the symptoms that can be approached
       directly
    B. Reducing patient anxiety
    C. Acclimating the patient to the therapeutic milieu
    D. Trying to get to know the patient quickly and
       acquiring an understanding of his emotional exper-
       iences
    E. To help the patient become emotionally involved
       with the other patients

18. Almost without exception, *most* dysfunctional families   18.____
    have a terrible time
    A. accepting responsibility for the primary patient's
       illness
    B. believing they are in therapy to help the primary
       patient
    C. overtly disagreeing about ways in which they see
       each other
    D. accepting the primary patient's illness
    E. accepting the help of the therapists

19. The particular outcome of a life crisis in an individual 19.____
    is MOST dependent upon the
    A. individual
    B. type of crisis
    C. duration of the crisis
    D. type of help received at the time of the crisis
    E. health of the individual prior to the crisis

20. *Which* of the following stages prepares the ground for the separation stage during the infancy period of development? The
    A. phase of symbiotic fusion
    B. autistic stage
    C. phase of individuation
    D. differentiation stage
    E. process of self control and self esteem

20.___

21. Therapeutic endeavors, in terms of a schizophrenic patient, are directed *primarily* toward
    A. those modes relying upon activities to convey a message
    B. external support and structure
    C. role playing
    D. provision of an identification figure
    E. verbal interaction

21.___

22. *When* do anxiety-reducing efforts *sometimes increase* anxiety?
    A. When the approach requires strengthening of defenses
    B. When the approach explores areas of conflict
    C. When the approach requires automatic response
    D. When the approach forces the patient to re-create conflicts
    E. Anxiety-reduction efforts never increase anxiety

22.___

23. *Which* of the following is, in effect, a compromise, expressing both an impulse and the defense against that impulse?
    A. Projection   B. Fantasy
    C. Identification   D. Symptom formation
    E. Defense mechanism

23.___

24. *What* is impression management? The process
    A. of creating a particular conception or image of oneself
    B. of creating an environment conducive to therapy
    C. by which the therapist creates an image of herself to meet the patient's needs
    D. by which the patient alters behavior through understanding
    E. of investigative therapy

24.___

25. *What* process is considered the *vehicle* of therapy?
    A. Mutual understanding of the therapeutic process
    B. The investigative approach required to gather the raw data of an experience
    C. The openness necessary to both hear and receive a message
    D. Repetition
    E. Communication

25.___

26. *Which* of the following is NOT a value of transference? 26.____
    It
    A. is a means of accomplishing improvement
    B. helps the patient develop a better relationship
       with others
    C. offers an opportunity for increased satisfaction
       and reality testing
    D. offers the patient an awareness of repetitive
       interactional patterns that may lead to cessation
       of this behavior
    E. allows the therapist the opportunity to force
       a re-experiencing of feelings and perceptions
       related to the figures in the patient's past

27. Prior to, and throughout the termination process, the 27.____
    patient must be made to have
    A. intellectual understanding integrated with awareness
    B. a clear perception of past and present reality
    C. realistic expectations
    D. confidence
    E. control over his behavior

28. *Which* phase of Group Therapy is the stage when the 28.____
    participants work on individual and collective dif-
    ficulties?
    A. Getting-acquainted stage
    B. Minor acting-out phase
    C. Major acting-out phase
    D. The stage when the group becomes a group
    E. Termination of the group stage

29. A Situation Model approach to the study of psychotherapy 29.____
    groups considers a significant group event as *one* that
    A. *changes* the groups' anxiety level, attitude, or
       behavior
    B. *catalyzes* feelings and responses
    C. *requires* therapist intervention
    D. *requires* therapist interaction
    E. *identifies* the groups' theme

30. Family Therapy is MOST successful *when* 30.____
    A. the family includes more than one psychotic member
    B. family members are motivated
    C. the family demonstrates fairly good social adjustment
    D. the primary patient is an adolescent or a young
       adult
    E. the family members are in reasonably good physical
       health

31. Communication occurs *when* 31.____
    A. a message is mutually understood by both the sender
       and the receiver
    B. the message received is understood on several
       levels at once
    C. both the sender and the receiver of a message
       understand their relationship to each other
    D. the clarifying metacommunications are congruous
       with the informational context of the message
    E. someone is in visual or auditory contact with
       another person

32. Hospitalized primary patients of Family Therapy Groups benefit MOST from
    A. exploratory therapy that furthers the patient's understanding of certain problematic feelings, thoughts, and behavior
    B. the free expression that takes place during the family conferences
    C. their relationships with personnel when everyone feels free enough to be himself
    D. the support derived from other patients who share common concerns and experiences
    E. the forgiving kind of relationships the hospital situation fosters

32.___

33. A very *basic* task in Family Therapy is teaching family members how to communicate clearly their
    A. goals   B. values
    C. fears   D. disagreements
    E. guilt or shame

33.___

34. *What* is the *most common* theme or relationship of all accidental crisis experiences?
    A. Conflict   B. Loss
    C. Responsibility   D. Guilt
    E. Regression

34.___

35. During *which* period of development is the concept of loss *most evident* to the individual? Stage of
    A. infancy   B. childhood
    C. adolescence   D. adulthood
    E. aging

35.___

36. All of the following are characteristics of any therapeutic undertaking EXCEPT
    A. planning   B. implementation
    C. diagnosis   D. intervention
    E. evaluation

36.___

37. *Which* of the following is TRUE of anxiety-reducing efforts? They
    A. are curative
    B. cause increased anxiety
    C. are effective only in a short-term sense
    D. are effective only in a long-term sense
    E. eliminate anxiety

37.___

38. Treating Symptom Formation *initially* requires
    A. stripping a patient of his defenses
    B. negating the patient's delusional system
    C. consideration of the nature and value of the symptom
    D. calling attention to the gains derived from the symptom
    E. having the patient identify his behavior as a symptom

38.___

39. *Why* is repetition really essential to investigative therapy?   39.___
    A. It provides structure
    B. Neither understanding nor retention can be relied upon
    C. It overcomes resistance
    D. It increases awareness
    E. It builds up tolerance to stress

40. *Which* of the following is considered the TOOL of therapy?   40.___
    A. Repetition   B. Clarity
    C. Communication   D. Validation
    E. Investigation

41. *Which* of the following statements is an example of   41.___
    countertransference?
    A. "I don't think he was my friend. Maybe that's what he is."
    B. "I feel guilty that she's sick because she's been worrying about me lately."
    C. "You're angry because I won't treat you like a sick child."
    D. "It's pretty clear that you're angry with me, but I'm not sure why."
    E. "She makes me mad; she acts just like my sister."

42. *Which* of the following is BASIC to understanding regres-   42.___
    sion? It
    A. indicates the patient is unwell
    B. is an unhealthy way of dealing with anxiety
    C. usually results from a single cause that can be worked out in therapy
    D. pre-supposes progress of one kind or another
    E. diminishes and usually disappears upon hospitalization

43. *What* is the *fundamental* tenet of group psychotherapy?
    To
    A. make the meaning in the interaction of the participants visible to them
    B. reduce anxiety through group support and interaction
    C. provide external support and structure through the identification figure of the therapist
    D. a level of group anxiety necessary to maintain focus on a specific issue
    E. provide for the development of more mature relationships

44. *Which* of the following areas of Situation Model approach   44.___
    to the study of psychotherapy groups is viewed in terms
    of emerging patterns?
    A. Therapist's intervention   B. Precipitating event
    C. Effects   D. Implications
    E. Focal event

45. *Why* is Family Therapy *one* of the *major* recognized   45.___
psychiatric treatment modalities? Families
    A. have tremendous influence in determining the
       eventual outcome of the treatment and rehabili-
       tation of psychiatric patients
    B. need to understand the difficulties of the
       primary patient
    C. are vital in helping the therapist understand
       the patient and his behavior
    D. are an important source of validation needed by
       the therapist to verify the correctness of
       established assumptions
    E. appear to carry factors enhancing regression within
       their boundaries

46. *Why* is Family Therapy NOT a *successful* form of treatment   46.___
when the family includes more than one psychotic member?
    A. Family members demonstrate too many inhibitions
       concerned with the identification and expression
       of feelings, wishes, and goals
    B. The family members interact and communicate in
       a disturbed way
    C. Family relationships are extremely tenacious and
       the family's defense formation is accentuated
       by the anxiety experienced during interpersonal
       confrontations
    D. The family member's level of communication is
       confused and understanding is obscured
    E. There is insufficient family strength for thera-
       peutic treatment

47. *What* is the PRIMARY focus of the weekly interdisciplinary 47.___
patient-staff meetings that occur during the hospitali-
zation phase of Family Therapy?
    A. Interpersonal aspects of community living
    B. Readjustment to the family environment
    C. Viewing family members in a more realistic way
    D. Exploration of the weekly family conferences
    E. Improving expression of feelings, wishes, and
       goals

48. A *reliable* indicator of interpersonal functioning is   48.___
    A. how the family members relate to each other
    B. the communication techniques the family members
       use
    C. the atmosphere of the home environment
    D. the nature of the messages exchanged among family
       members
    E. how the family responds to treatment

49. *What* is the *most important* aspect of self-awareness?　　49.____
Helping patients to
    A. identify their feelings
    B. translate feelings into terms that can be understood by others
    C. deal with conflict in a more healthy, less defeating manner
    D. accept the responsibility for what they feel, including the consequences of their behavior
    E. understand why they act as they do so that more effective behavior can be adopted

50. When the primary patient does not or cannot verbalize　　50.____
for himself during a family conference, the nurse
should
    A. urge the patient to talk
    B. allow other family members to talk for the patient
    C. accept the patient's silence
    D. support the patient by expressing her own feelings when they correspond to those of the patient
    E. allow the patient to return to the ward

KEY (CORRECT ANSWERS)

1.	C	11.	C	21.	E	31.	E	41.	E
2.	C	12.	A	22.	B	32.	C	42.	D
3.	E	13.	B	23.	D	33.	D	43.	A
4.	B	14.	E	24.	A	34.	B	44.	D
5.	E	15.	E	25.	B	35.	E	45.	A
6.	D	16.	A	26.	E	36.	D	46.	C
7.	A	17.	D	27.	C	37.	C	47.	A
8.	A	18.	C	28.	D	38.	C	48.	B
9.	E	19.	D	29.	A	39.	B	49.	D
10.	B	20.	C	30.	D	40.	C	50.	D

EXAMINATION SECTION

DIRECTIONS: Each question or incomplete statement is followed by several suggested answers or completions. Select the one that BEST answers the question or completes the statement. PRINT THE LETTER OF THE CORRECT ANSWER IN THE SPACE AT THE RIGHT.

1. All of the following are true of the dyadic relationship EXCEPT: 1.___
   A. The goal is to further the patient's understanding of certain problematic feelings, thoughts, and behavior
   B. A critical assessment of the patient's area of impairment must be made
   C. An overall plan for patients with similar behavior should be developed
   D. Nursing intervention must consider the strengths which the patient has at his disposal
   E. It is through avenues of integration that the nurse approaches her task of improving the patient's total functioning

2. *What* is essential to the principle of anxiety reduction?   2.___
   A. Exploring areas of conflict
   B. Strengthening defenses
   C. To allow anxiety to reach a level that facilitates review of experience
   D. To initiate new behavior to reduce anxiety
   E. To assist the patient to develop means of dealing with conflict

3. *What* is the BEST approach for treating a symptom that results in compulsive behavior?   3.___
   A. Forbidding the compulsive behavior
   B. Preventing the compulsive behavior
   C. Calling attention to the gains derived from the compulsive behavior
   D. Encouraging the patient to direct his effort toward reducing or eliminating aspects of the behavior
   E. Calling attention to the difficulties resulting from the compulsive behavior

4. When evasion is identified in patient communication, the nurse *should*   4.___
   A. insist on specificity through a consistent focus upon an ever-narrowing issue
   B. prohibit expansion to a wider frame of reference
   C. increase the patient's level of anxiety
   D. change the subject
   E. respond with generalizations to reduce anxiety

5. Counter transference is based on   5.___
   - A. generalizations   B. therapeutic despair
   - C. unresolved conflicts   D. anxiety
   - E. projection

6. *Which* of the following are TRUE OF regressive behavior?   6.___
   It
   - I. can occur even when other parts of the personality are functioning productively
   - II. is endorsed behavior in some situations and circumstances
   - III. is rarely a way of gaining attention
   - IV. always carries over from one setting to another
   - V. accompanies both mental and physical illness

   The CORRECT answer is:
   - A. I, III, V   B. II, IV, V   C. II, III, IV
   - D. I, II, V   E. II, III, IV, V

7. *Why* do the phases of Group Therapy occur again and   7.___
   again? It is due to
   - A. pseudo-working relationships
   - B. the manifestation of anxiety
   - C. collective regression
   - D. old members leaving and new members being introduced
   - E. the behavior of deviates

8. *What* is the CHIEF benefit of a Situation Model approach   8.___
   to the study of psychotherapy groups? It
   - A. is less time-consuming
   - B. is a means of synthesizing a vast amount of data
   - C. is a means of keeping verbatim accounts
   - D. ensures validity of data reported
   - E. precludes further data analysis

9. All of the following are qualities that indicate favor-   9.___
   able response to family therapy EXCEPT:
   - A. Family members have a basic interest in the welfare of one another
   - B. Family members demonstrate a fairly good social adjustment prior to the identified illness of one member
   - C. Indications that family members are in reasonably good physical health
   - D. Evidence that the problems presented belong to either a nuclear or extended family
   - E. Indications that one member functions as a catalyst for therapeutic change in the family

10. Communication becomes obscure and problems of confusion   10.___
and misunderstanding result *when*
    A. communication does not define what the message
       is about
    B. the receiver of the message does not indicate
       his relationship with the sender
    C. the clarifying metacommunications are not congruous
       with the informational context of the message
    D. communication does not pertain to present reality
    E. metacommunications are absent

11. *What* is the CHIEF importance of the Family Therapy   11.___
Unit's nursing leader? To
    A. *create* an atmosphere that is conducive to a free
       exchange of feelings and ideas among the staff
       which will carry over to the therapeutic milieu
    B. *set-up and maintain* the type of relationship
       that stimulate the relationships patients might
       experience outside the hospital
    C. *communicate* certain expectations of all family
       members to the staff
    D. *recognize* the different skills and talents of
       the staff
    E. *clarify* for the psychiatric interdisciplinary
       team the kinds of contributions nurses can reason-
       ably be expected to make

12. *What* is the MOST serious *negative* feature of multi-   12.___
disciplinary co-therapy?
    A. Disagreement   B. Lack of mutual respect
    C. Personality clash   D. Domination
    E. Competitiveness

13. *What* is necessary to achieve a healthy resolution to   13.___
a loss?
    A. Therapeutic intervention
    B. Psychologic maturity
    C. An adequate mourning experience
    D. Achieving a healthy self-image
    E. Problem-solving ability

14. *Which* of the following are developmental tasks of the   14.___
period of childhood?
    I. Differentiation is made between self and others
   II. Attachments to parents begin to dissolve
  III. Ability to deal with some of the external demands
       of society
   IV. Learning to win recognition through the process
       of production and mastery
   V. Learning to appreciate a sex role and developing
       a personal sense of value
The CORRECT answer is:
    A. I, V   B. I, II, V   C. I, II, IV
    D. II, III, IV   E. II, III, V

15. *Which* of the following represent crisis situations?   15.___
    I. The attempt ot engage in intimate relationships
   II. Pregnancy
  III. Loss of occupation
   IV. Reduction in prestige and income
    V. Coming to "terms" with your own body
The CORRECT answer is:
  A. I, III, IV   B. II, III, IV   C. II, V
  D. III, IV, V   E. All of the above

16. *What* is necessary for a dyadic relationship to succeed? 16.___
The
  A. patient must be able to communicate thoughts or
    beliefs in a comprehensible manner
  B. patient must be able to understand his problematic
    feelings, thoughts, and behavior
  C. patient must be able to review his experiences
    and derive new meanings
  D. patient must be aware of the environment and purpose
    of the treatment
  E. patient must desire treatment

17. *What* is the value of a patient's re-creation of conflict? 17.___
It
  A. aids in the creation of an anxiety-free environment
  B. strengthens **defenses**
  C. aids in the identification of conflict
  D. reduces patient discomfort
  E. aids in planning and implementing intervention

18. *Which* of the following is of *particular* interest in 18.___
investigative therapy? The
  A. response of others to the patient
  B. patient's awareness of his behavior
  C. patient's goals
  D. manner in which the patient presents himself
  E. affect of the environment on the patient

19. *What* element of distortion exists in tranference? The 19.___
  A. patient disguises certain aspects of self that
    are deemed unacceptable
  B. patient tries to obtain responses of a specific
    nature from others to reinforce self-deception
  C. patient's perceptions and reactions do not pertain
    to past or present reality
  D. therapist assumes a role complementary to the
    patient's that fosters maintenance of existing
    patterns
  E. therapist invests the patient with certain character-
    istics that do not pertain to present reality

20. *Which* of the following decide toleration and alteration   20.___
    of regressive behavior?
      I. Who is exhibiting the behavior
     II. The cause of the behavior
    III. How long the behavior will be tolerated
     IV. Where the behavior will be allowed to occur
      V. The ways and means of intervention
    The CORRECT answer is:
      A. I, II, V   B. I, II, III, IV   C. III, IV, V
      D. I,IV   E. I, V

21. *Which* of the following is NOT TRUE of Family Therapy   21.___
    guidelines?
      A. Conferences are held once a week during the primary
         patient's hospitalization
      B. Conferences are held more than once a week when
         the family is on an out-patient basis
      C. Conferences include family members over the age
         of five who live with him
      D. A family group should consist of at least three
         people, including the primary patient
      E. Conferences are usually conducted by two co-thera-
         pists who represent different psychiatric disciplines

22. *What* is ESSENTIAL to establishing satisfactory relation-   22.___
    ships with other people?
      A. Honesty
      B. Respect
      C. Appreciation of the feelings of others
      D. Clear communication
      E. Understanding how one's own behavior affects the
         responses of others

23. *Which* of the following is NOT TRUE of the philosophy   23.___
    of the Family Therapy Unit during the hospitalization
    of the primary patient?
      A. The period of hospitalization should be as brief
         as possible
      B. Hospitalization should be viewed as a way to assist
         families in dealing with their life situations
      C. The therapeutic goal is having a patient assume
         total responsibility for his behavior
      D. The amount of responsibility a patient is able
         or willing to assume is a constantly changing
         thing
      E. Patient privileges such as ground passes, telephone
         use, etc., are limited or restricted as part of
         an intensive, temporary measure

24. Unsuccessful or drop-out cases from Family Therapy   24.___
are often the result of
    I. lack of motivation and commitment on the family's
       part
   II. lack of skill of the therapists
  III. a severe degree of family pathology
   IV exaggerated interpersonal deprivation of the primary
      patient
    V. the discharge of the primary patient before long-
      range therapeutic goals have been met
The CORRECT answer is:
   A. I, V   B. I, III, IV   C. III, IV, V
   D. II, III, IV, V   E. I, II, III, IV

25. During the process of grief, *what* occurs after denial   25.___
of the unendurable reality?
   A. Ignoring the loss
   B. Transference of affection
   C. Development of awareness of the pain and emptiness
      caused by the loss
   D. Development of a meaningful object relationship
   E. Rejection of the emptiness caused by the loss

26. *Which* of the following periods of development has the   26.___
greatest potential for learning and sharing?
   A. Infancy   B. Childhood
   C. Adolescence   D. Young adulthood
   E. Adulthood

27. *What* type of solidarity exists in a mother-child relation- 27.___
ship or a husband-wife relationship? _____ solidarity.
   A. Horizontal   B. Generational
   C. Mutual   D. Vertical
   E. Functional

28. During the course of a dyadic relationship, the therapist 28.___
   A. increases the patient's awareness without involving
      the boundaries of her own awareness
   B. should reveal her own feelings of hopelessness
      and helplessness
   C. should ignore her own feelings of anxiety while
      increasing the patient's ability to cope with his
   D. should maintain objectivity at the same time as
      she increases her involvement with the patient
   E. should direct all the operations of therapy only
      toward the patient and not toward herself

29. *What* is the BEST way for an individual to deal with   29.___
anxiety? To
   A. seek an anxiety-free environment
   B. maintain it within a functional range
   C. initiate adaptive behavior
   D. confront the source
   E. ignore it

30. *Which* of the following is TRUE of symptom formation?   30.__
    It
    A. is a mechanism that effectively diminishes anxiety
       and experiences encountered in the past
    B. is an inefficient and restrictive means of coping
       with adaptional problems
    C. is ineffective in achieving a balance between
       the polar elements of conflict
    D. is an effective means of coping with adaptional
       problems
    E. helps control feelings, thoughts, and actions
       essential to integrated behavior

31. Immediate intervention is required during investigative   31.__
    therapy to
    A. allow the patient to achieve specific goals in
       relation to his own desires and conflicts
    B. alter the efforts of personnel toward the long-
       term goal
    C. meet the patient's needs
    D. predict behavior
    E. prevent dependency on past behavior

32. An exploratory approach to therapy is unrealistic for   32.__
    all of the following reasons EXCEPT: The patient is
    unable to
    A. *focus* attention
    B. *use* abstractions
    C. *relate* present and past experience
    D. *generalize* appropriately
    E. *acknowledge* certain aspects of behavior and experience

33. When the therapist, through countertransference, assumes   33.__
    a role complementary to the patient's, it
    A. *provides for* constructive interaction
    B. *allows* therapeutic aims to be enhanced
    C. *aids in* the development of appropriate intervention
    D. *fosters* maintenance of existing patterns
    E. *encourages* the patient's expression of feelings
       and thoughts

34. All of the following are TRUE of regression EXCEPT: It   34.__
    A. is a positive sign of mental health as a way of
       dealing with anxiety
    B. involves inner suffering and social visibility
    C. can be unhealthy if it doesn't occur
    D. does not always carry over from one setting to
       another
    E. diminishes and usually disappears upon hospitali-
       zation

35. *What* information for a Situation Model approach to
    the study of psychotherapy groups is included in the
    area of Group Dynamics? The
    A. background information that seems significantly
       related to the focal point
    B. pertinent group interaction, group themes, and
       level of group anxiety at the time of the focal
       event
    C. individual motivations and behavior related to
       the focal event
    D. therapist's participation in the focal event
    E. therapist's response to the focal event

36. *What* is the *overall objective* of Family Therapy? To
    A. identify, clarify, **and correct disturbed ways**
       in which family members communicate and interact
    B. analyze interpersonal progress
    C. have family members revise their earlier distortions
       about the others
    D. identify the cause of the primary patient's symptoms
       and to formulate a pattern of response
    E. have family members identify positively with the
       hospitalized member and contribute to his recovery

37. Every communication defines both what the message is
    about *and*
    A. how it is understood
    B. if it is understood
    C. how the sender conceives of his relationship with
       the receiver
    D. how the receiver conceives of his relationship
       with the sender
    E. the general or specific context in which an inter-
       action takes place

38. When a patient behaves destructively and indicates
    an impaired ability to communicate clearly, the nurse
    should
    A. *place* the patient in restraints
    B. *calm* the patient and talk to him
    C. *limit* the patient's destructive behavior and insist
       that he extend himself as far as he can to express
       himself in a more useful and clear way
    D. *restrain* the patient's destructive behavior and
       accept his unclear messages until he is better
       able to communicate
    E. *allow* the destructive behavior within the limits
       of safety and, afterwards, question the validity
       of the patient's perception that inspired it

35.____

36.____

37.____

38.____

39. *What* is the FIRST step to occur if successful grieving is to be achieved?
    A. Acceptance of the unendurable reality
    B. Denial of the unendurable reality
    C. Acceptance of the emptiness caused by the loss
    D. Development of an awareness to the pain of the loss
    E. Ignoring the loss

39.___

40. The amount of trust derived from earliest infantile experience *mostly* depends on the
    A. strength of the mother's ego
    B. infant's innate instinctual apparatus and the mother's past relational expectations for the child
    C. absolute quantities of food
    D. demonstrations of love
    E. quality of the maternal relationship

40.___

41. *What* is *necessary* for verbal communication to succeed?
    A. Collecting data
    B. Minimizing resistance
    C. Renewing experience
    D. Comprehension of behavior
    E. Tolerance of stress

41.___

42. At the beginning of the termination process, the therapist's efforts are directed *toward*
    A. the prevention of grief
    B. expression of emotions that indicate the patient's feeling toward separation
    C. having the patient concentrate upon the theme of strength
    D. having the patient view the separation in an abstract manner
    E. having the patient understand the separation

42.___

43. *What* use does a Situation Model approach have for the study of psychotherapy groups?
    A. It identifies emerging patterns and cause-effect relationships in group development
    B. It evaluates the progress of the group
    C. It finds meaning in group events and individual behavior
    D. It helps in planning and evaluating therapeutic intervention
    E. All of the above

43.___

44. *What* are metacommunications?
    A. Messages that are understood in the context of the communication
    B. Nonverbal communication
    C. The specific factual information contained in the message
    D. All aspects of communication including the specific factual information contained in the message
    E. All aspects of communication excluding the specific factual information contained in the message

44.___

45. *Which* of the following is NOT an advantage in using   45.___
    co-therapists in Family Therapy?
    A. It provides a greater amount of support for indi-
       vidual members of a family group
    B. Feelings of competitiveness arise between the
       therapists
    C. They may express their disagreements with each
       other during the conferences
    D. One co-therapist may support one member of the
       family while the other co-therapist simultaneously
       supports another during the conferences
    E. They divide the task of private interviewing

46. During Family Therapy the dysfuntional technique of   46.___
    disqualification is *most often* used *when*
    A. parents respond inconsistently
    B. clarifying metacommunications are not congruous
       with the informational context of the message
    C. members have such low self-esteen they cannot
       see themselves as important enough to have an
       influence over the response of others
    D. members fear the possibility of rejection or
       retaliation if they communicate more clearly
    E. agreement cannot be reached and disagreement can-
       not be tolerated

47. *Which* of the following is a response to a loss that   47.___
    is *basically* rooted in fantasy?
    A. Grief   B. Disorientation
    C. Mourning   D. Depression
    E. Regression

48. *What* is the PRIMARY task of the adolescent period of   48.___
    development?
    A. Learning to win recognition through the process
       of production and mastery
    B. Development of a sense of identity
    C. The process of differentiation from parents
    D. Finding an emotional investment in something out-
       side of oneself
    E. Development of self-control and self-esteem

49. *Which* phase of group therapy is the stage when extreme   49.___
    deviates have been removed and productive activity
    resumes?
    A. Getting-acquainted stage
    B. Minor acting-out phase
    C. Crescendo-of-tension phase
    D. The stage when the group becomes a group
    E. Termination of the group stage

11

50. *What* phase of group therapy *usually* causes the most
disequilibrium within the group?
    A. Getting-acquainted stage
    B. Minor acting-out phase
    C. Major acting-out phase
    D. The stage when the group becomes a group
    E. Termination of the group stage

50.___

KEY (CORRECT ANSWERS)

1. C	11. A	21. B	31. B	41. B
2. B	12. E	22. D	32. E	42. B
3. E	13. C	23. E	33. D	43. E
4. A	14. D	24. E	34. E	44. E
5. C	15. E	25. C	35. B	45. B
6. D	16. A	26. B	36. A	46. E
7. D	17. E	27. D	37. C	47. D
8. B	18. D	28. D	38. C	48. D
9. D	19. C	29. C	39. B	49. C
10. C	20. C	30. B	40. E	50. E

EXAMINATION SECTION
TEST 1

DIRECTIONS: Each question or incomplete statement is followed by several suggested answers or completions. Select the one that BEST answers the question or completes the statement. *PRINT THE LETTER OF THE CORRECT ANSWER IN THE SPACE AT THE RIGHT.*

1. Which one of the following "suggestions to interviewers" should be AVOIDED?　　　　1.____

    A. Encourage the client to verbalize his thoughts and feelings.
    B. Cover as much as possible in each interview.
    C. Don't hesitate to refer the client to someone else who might be more helpful in the situation.
    D. The problem which is presented initially, or the one which seems most obvious, often is not the real one.

2. If it seems clear that disturbance in parents' marital relationships is a major factor in causing a child to be emotionally disturbed, the counselor should　　　　2.____

    A. point this out to the parents and tell them that for the welfare of their children, they should resolve their difficulties
    B. suggest that he will be willing to discuss their marital difficulties with them
    C. ignore this and concentrate on helping the child
    D. tactfully suggest that their marital difficulties may be playing a part in their child's disturbance and offer to refer the parents to a qualified marriage counseling service

3. The process of collecting, analyzing, synthesizing and interpreting information about the client should be　　　　3.____

    A. completed prior to counseling
    B. completed early in the counseling process
    C. limited to counseling which is primarily diagnostic in purpose
    D. continuous throughout counseling

4. Catharsis, the "emotional unloading" of the client's feelings, has a value in the early stages of counseling because it accomplishes all BUT which one of the following goals?　　　　4.____

    A. It relieves strong physiological tensions in the client.
    B. It increases the client's anxiety and therefore his motivation to continue counseling.
    C. It provides a verbal substitute for "acting out" the client's aggressive feelings.
    D. It releases emotional energy which the client has been using to maintain his defenses.

5. During the first interview, the counselor can expect the client to participate at his BEST when the counselor　　　　5.____

    A. structures the nature of the counseling process
    B. attempts to summarize the client's problem for him
    C. allows the client to verbalize at his own pace
    D. tells the client that he understands the presenting problem

6. To obtain the most effective results in change of attitude and behavior through parent education, the leader should be

    A. thoroughly grounded in the whole field of psychology
    B. able to help members of the group look at their own attitudes and behavior in constructive ways
    C. completely confident as to the right solution to problems that may be brought up
    D. a warm, charming, friendly human being

6.____

7. A social worker's report about a client states that a mother has ambivalent feelings concerning her child. This means that the mother

    A. has contradictory emotional reactions concerning her child
    B. is overprotective of the child
    C. strongly rejects the child
    D. is unduly apprehensive about the child's welfare

7.____

8. A psychological report notes, "The client shows little effect." This means that the client

    A. did not take the test too seriously
    B. did not show emotional behavior in situations which normally call for such reactions
    C. did not show signs of fatigue as the testing progressed
    D. reacted to the test situation in a generally favorable manner

8.____

9. A psychologist's report states, in part, that a client exhibits some masochistic symptoms. This will be evident to the counselor through the client's persistent attempts at

    A. self-assertion
    B. self-effacement
    C. inflicting physical harm on others
    D. sexual molestation of others of the same sex

9.____

10. According to research studies, the type of counselor response that is MOST often followed by a client's expression of insight or illumination is

    A. clarification of feeling
    B. reflection of feeling
    C. simple acceptance
    D. exploratory question

10.____

11. Of the following, the BEST way to deal with a 12-year-old boy who feels inferior to his peers is to

    A. provide tasks which he can master with little difficulty
    B. show him how irrational his feelings are
    C. accept his declarations of lack of confidence sympathetically
    D. carefully arrange situations in which he will be obliged to show leadership

11.____

12. In counseling or psychotherapy, the factor which is the MOST important for success tends to be the

    A. counselor's theoretical orientation
    B. counselor's attitudes and feelings toward the client

12.____

C. techniques used by the counselor

D. amount of experience and training possessed by the counselor

13. Transference is an important aspect of   13._____

    A. test construction   B. grade placement

    C. anecdotal record keeping   D. therapy

14. The MOST desirable way of establishing rapport with a client who comes to the counse-   14._____
lor with a problem is to

    A. demonstrate sincere interest in him

    B. offer to do everything possible to solve his problem for him

    C. use the language of the client

    D. promise to keep his problem confidential

15. Role playing has been used as a technique in parent education work. Of the following,   15._____
the major value is that it

    A. permits parents to express unconscious feelings and thereby solve conflicts

    B. tells a story in a forceful and therefore lasting way

    C. provides an opportunity for the individual to view his problems by standing off and
looking at them through the eyes of someone else

    D. brings to light problems people never knew they had

16. If during a counseling situation a client expressed anger about a particular situation,   16._____
which of the following responses would a non-directive counselor MOST likely make?

    A. "Why are you so angry?"

    B. "Is there any need to get so upset about this?"

    C. "This has really made you very mad, hasn't it?"

    D. "Do you feel better now that you have expressed your anger?"

17. In a counseling process, the counselor should usually give information   17._____

    A. whenever it is needed

    B. at the end of the process

    C. in the introductory interview

    D. just before the client would ordinarily request it

18. "After having recognized and clarified feelings and conflicts, it is usually necessary to go   18._____
beyond the stage of understanding and to elaborate a constructive plan for future action."
Which of the following people would NOT go along with the above statement?

    A. Thorne   B. Robinson

    C. Williamson   D. Rogers

19. The counselor should focus his attention in the beginning upon   19._____

    A. the transference phenomenon

    B. evidences of hostility

    C. the unique characteristics of the particular relationship at hand

    D. indications of client aggressiveness

20. A recent guidance text that stresses the broad developments of our national heritage, our contemporary social setting, our value patterns, and also the integration into guidance of many disciplines-sociology, anthropology, philosophy, psychology-is

    A. FOUNDATIONS OF GUIDANCE - Miller
    B. GUIDANCE POLICY AND PRACTICE - Mathewson
    C. GUIDANCE IN TODAY'S SCHOOLS - Mortenson & Schmuller
    D. GUIDANCE SERVICES - Humphreys, Traxler & North

21. Which one of the following characteristics of counseling is inconsistent with the others?

    A. Counseling is more than advice-giving.
    B. Counseling involves something more than the solution to an immediate problem.
    C. Counseling concerns itself with attitudes rather than actions.
    D. Counseling involves intellectual rather than emotional attitudes as its basic raw material.

22. One approach to counseling has been labeled "non-directive". The word "non-directive" derives from the fact that, in this approach to counseling, the counselor

    A. does not tell the client what he should do
    B. makes the client responsible for the direction of the course of the interviews
    C. does not make judgments about the behavior of the client
    D. avoids possible areas of threat to the client

23. Of the following personality traits, which would be LEAST essential for an effective counselor to possess?

    A. Extroversion   B. Objectivity
    C. Security   D. Sensitivity

24. Interpretation as a therapeutic tool is considered a hindrance to therapy progress by

    A. orthodox Freudians   B. neo-analysts
    C. Rogerians   D. Adlerians

25. The current interpersonal behavior of the client is probably MOST important as a therapy topic to which two analytic theorists?

    A. Freud and Adler   B. Adler and Rank
    C. Freud and Rank   D. Horney and Sullivan

KEY (CORRECT ANSWERS)

1.	B	11.	A
2.	D	12.	B
3.	D	13.	D
4.	B	14.	A
5.	C	15.	C
6.	B	16.	C
7.	A	17.	A
8.	B	18.	D
9.	B	19.	C
10.	C	20.	A

21.	D
22.	B
23.	A
24.	C
25.	D

———

TEST 2

DIRECTIONS: Each question or incomplete statement is followed by several suggested answers or completions. Select the one that BEST answers the question or completes the statement. *PRINT THE LETTER OF THE CORRECT ANSWER IN THE SPACE AT THE RIGHT.*

1. When a counselor is listening to a client, it is MOST important that he be able to   1.____

    A. show interest and agreement with what the client is saying
    B. paraphrase what the client is saying
    C. understand the significance of what the client is saying
    D. differentiate between fact and fiction in what the client is saying

2. On which one of the following is successful counseling LEAST likely to depend?   2.____

    A. The counselor's theoretical orientation
    B. The counselor's ability to bring the client's feelings and attitudes into the open
    C. The counselor's diagnostic ability
    D. The client's readiness for counseling

3. A client is referred to you for counseling against his will and is suspicious and uncooper-   3.____
ative. You should

    A. explain to him that you cannot help him unless he is prepared to cooperate
    B. explain that you are not taking sides and that you will be impartial
    C. show him that you know how he feels and encourage him to talk about it
    D. explain that you are on his side and will listen sympathetically to anything that he might care to bring up

4. Which one of the following would NOT be considered a basic objective of the first inter-   4.____
view between a client and a counselor?

    A. Beginning a sound counseling relationship
    B. Identifying the client's real problem
    C. Opening up the area of client feelings and attitudes
    D. Clarifying the nature of the counseling process for the client

5. All of the following counselor statements or actions are appropriate techniques for ending   5.____
an interview EXCEPT

    A. "Our time is nearly up. Is there something else you have in mind for today?"
    B. "Let's see now. Suppose we go over what we've accomplished today."
    C. Counselor may glance at his watch and say, "When would you like to come in again?"
    D. Counselor may shuffle papers on desk and say, "Now, let's see; when is my next appointment?"

6. It has been recognized in recent literature that the value structure of the individual coun-   6.____
selor has what kind of effect on the counseling process?

    A. Direct   B. Indirect
    C. Little   D. None

7. The intensive study of the same individuals over a fairly long period of time represents the

    A. cross-sectional approach   B. longitudinal approach
    C. clinical approach   D. biographical approach

7.____

8. Of the following techniques, the one which is MOST characteristic of non-directive or client-centered therapy is

    A. encouraging transference
    B. free association
    C. reflection of feeling
    D. permissive questioning

8.____

9. In making predictions about how a client will behave in a given situation, a counselor

    A. should limit himself to those situations for which "actuarial" data are available
    B. must rely on "clinical" judgment in many situations but use "actuarial" data wherever possible
    C. should rely on "clinical" judgment in all situations, since they are more valid than "actuarial" predictions
    D. always uses "actuarial" data, but modifies them in light of his "clinical" impression of the client

9.____

10. A research study that establishes an hypothesis, sets up control groups, collects data, and generalizes from the data is

    A. formulative   B. diagnostic
    C. experimental   D. exploratory

10.____

11. The MOST usable single index of the social and economic status of all the members of any family is

    A. occupation of the father
    B. religious affiliation of the family
    C. location of the home in the community
    D. socio-economic rating by neighbors

11.____

12. When a counselor does NOT understand the meaning of a response that a counselee has made, the counselor usually should

    A. proceed to another topic
    B. admit his lack of understanding and ask for clarification
    C. act as if he understands so that the counselee's confidence in him is not shaken
    D. ask the counselee to choose his words more carefully

12.____

13. When the counselor makes a response which touches off a high degree of resistance in the counselee, he should

    A. apologize and rephrase his remark in a less threatening manner
    B. accept the resistance
    C. ignore the counselee's resistance
    D. recognize that little more will be accomplished in the interview and offer another appointment

13.____

14. Directive and non-directive counseling are two emphases in counseling theory and prac-   14.____
    tice. From the pairs of names listed below, indicate the two that are representative of the
    Directive school.

    A. Thorne and Williamson   B. Rogers and Thorne
    C. Williamson and Sullivan   D. Sullivan and Rogers

15. Rogerian counseling theory is based on the assumption that the potential and tendency   15.____
    for growth toward a fully functioning personality is present in

    A. a few "self-actualized" persons
    B. most people of above average intelligence
    C. people whose behavior can be considered as "normal" and socially effective
    D. all people

16. Anecdotal records should contain which type(s) of information?   16.____

    A. Evaluations   B. Interpretations
    C. Factual reports   D. Prognoses

17. RESISTANCE in relation to psychological counseling typically refers to the   17.____

    A. client's defenses against his inner conflicts
    B. counselor's unwillingness to deal with the client's emotional problems
    C. client's having enough ego strength so that he can face his problems
    D. counselor's having enough ego strength so that he can help the client face his
        problems

18. On which one of the following does the democratic leader specifically rely? His ability to   18.____

    A. listen and tactfully guide the discussion in the direction he has planned and the
        members' willingness to cooperate
    B. diagnose situations, to interpret and explain them to the members and their willing-
        ness to accept
    C. discern the issues which the members could profitably discuss and his willingness
        to allow them with his help to do so
    D. understand the meaning of the response from the member's frame of reference
        and his willingness for them to make decisions

19. Advisement in counseling is MOST effective when the counselee is in a state of   19.____

    A. perceiving his problem as related to a conflict with inner forces
    B. minimal conflict and of optimal readiness for action
    C. perceiving his problem as related to an external conflict
    D. feeling extremely ambivalent about his self-concept

20. Of the following, the MOST valid use of projective techniques is the study of the   20.____

    A. problems which an individual faces
    B. cultural effects upon an individual
    C. inner world of an individual
    D. human relationships of an individual

21. Diagnosis is NOT regarded as a helpful antecedent to counseling by 21.____

    A. Cottle   B. Rogers
    C. Thorne   D. Williamson

22. The beginning counselor must be alert to interferences to rapport. Which one of the following is NOT considered an intereference? 22.____

    A. Injecting the counselor's present mood
    B. Engaging in "small talk" at the start of the interview
    C. Registering surprise or dismay
    D. Emphasizing the counselor's ability

23. There is some evidence according to Rogers that counseling is more effective with 23.____

    A. younger adults or higher intelligence
    B. older adults of higher intelligence
    C. younger adults of lower intelligence
    D. older adults of lower intelligence

24. In assisting with the scheduling of interviews for educational planning, the counselor should suggest that group instruction 24.____

    A. follow the counseling interview
    B. is not necessary when individual interviews can be scheduled since each case is different
    C. precede the counseling
    D. may either precede or follow the counseling interview

25. A client has requested an interview with the counselor to discuss a personal problem. In general, the BEST way to begin the interview is to 25.____

    A. come directly to the point and encourage the client to talk about his problem
    B. assure him that everything discussed will be confidential
    C. offer to help him in every way possible
    D. inquire whether he has discussed the problem with anyone else

KEY (CORRECT ANSWERS)

1.	C		11.	A
2.	A		12.	B
3.	C		13.	B
4.	B		14.	A
5.	D		15.	D
6.	A		16.	C
7.	B		17.	A
8.	C		18.	C
9.	B		19.	B
10.	C		20.	C

21.	B
22.	B
23.	A
24.	C
25.	A

plain talk about...

WifeAbuse

- "To have and to hold...to love and to cherish..."
- "Be it ever so humble, there's no place like home."

These sentiments reflect the feelings of most people towards marriage, home, and family—but not all. The surprising fact is that a lot of violence, bringing fear and pain, is reported among family members.

For example, about one-quarter of all murders in the United States take place within the family. Surveys of American couples show that 20 to 50 percent have suffered violence regularly in their marriages. The records indicate that between two and four million incidents of domestic violence occur every single year. Wife abuse is one kind of family violence that probably occurs far more often than most people imagine. The tragedy is that many women suffer this abuse for years without getting help. This flier explores what wife abuse is, who experiences it, some reasons it occurs, the pattern it usually takes, and why women don't get help. Finally, it looks at what women can do if they are abused and how, ultimately, the abuse might be prevented.

What Do We Mean by "Wife Abuse"?

Defining wife abuse or wife battering is not easy. For starters, whom are we thinking of when we use the word "wife"? Actually, any woman who maintains an intimate relationship with a man (her husband, ex-husband, boyfriend or lover) could become a battered or abused "wife." The words "abused" or "battered" which are used here do not refer to the normal conflict and stress that occur in all close relationships, but rather to the violence that can cause serious injury and death. In the pamphlet, "Assaults on women: rape and wife-beating," Natalie Jaffe cites a typical description of the kind of physical harm suffered by battered women surveyed in shelters and treatment in California.

"Most injuries were to the head and neck and, in addition to bruises, strangle marks, black eyes, and split lips, resulted in eye damage, fractured jaws, broken noses, and permanent hearing loss. Assaults to the trunk of the body were almost as common and produced a broken collarbone, bruised and broken ribs, a fractured tailbone, internal hemorrhaging, and a lacerated liver."

These are serious consequences of serious assaults. Another serious aspect is that once wife beating occurs, it is likely to happen again and again, with violence getting worse over time.

A Closer Look at How the Abused Woman Feels

A woman who has been abused over a long period of time is afraid. Not only is she afraid that she, herself, will be seriously hurt, but if she has children, she fears for their safety also. Her feelings of fear link her to all other women, from all classes of society, in similar situations.

Fear might be a woman's first and most immediate feeling during or after a beating, but other negative feelings may surface when she is not in physical danger. The abused woman is apt to develop doubts about herself. She might wonder if she is justified in fearing for her life and calling herself an "abused wife." Most likely, however, a woman who thinks or feels she is being abused, probably is.

Or, she may feel guilty, even though she's done nothing wrong. An abused wife may feel responsible for her husband's violence because in some way she may have provoked him. This has her placing the shame and blame on herself—instead of her abuser. The longer she puts up with the abuse and does nothing to avoid or prevent it, the less she likes herself. Along with the feeling of being a failure, both as a woman and in her marriage, may come a real feeling of being trapped and powerless, with no way out.

Why Do Men Abuse Their Wives?

Instances of wife abuse have been on record in the United States since the 1830s, but only every now and then does it arouse public concern. Generally, public opinion supports traditional family relations and male authority. The battering syndrome is both cause and effect of stereotyped roles and the unequal power relations between men and women. No social class is exempt. Wife abuse occurs in wealthy as well as in poor communities—in middle class as well as in working class families. Over the years it has been tolerated by those who govern community affairs, the courts, medicine, psychiatry, police, schools, and the church. History shows that the helping professions often protected patterns of family authority, unwittingly sanctioning wife abuse rather than condemning it.

1

Other Factors

Present-day society is one in which violence in the movies, on TV, and in the newspapers is familiar and accepted. Many husbands who abuse their wives have learned that violence, especially against women, is okay. They often were abused themselves as children or saw their mothers abused. The battered wife most likely grew up in a similar environment.

There are other psychological reasons. A wife abuser tends to be filled with anger, resentment, suspicion, and tension. He also, underneath all his aggressive behavior, can be insecure and feel like a loser. He may use violence to give vent to the bad feelings he has about himself or his lot in life. Home is one place he can express those feelings without punishment to himself. If he were angry with his boss and struck him, he would pay the price. But all too often he gets away without penalty when he beats his wife. She becomes the target of his vengeance, and he gets the satisfaction he's looking for.

What about the victimized wife? If she accepts her husband's traditional male authority, she may be labeled as immature. If she fights back or if she refuses to sleep with him if he's drunk, she might be accused of being hostile, domineering, and masculine. These are complaints of abused women.

Patterns

Familiar patterns of wife abuse often develop in three phases: the tension-building phase, the explosion or the actual beating phase, and the loving phase. The tension builds over a series of small occurrences such as a wife's request for money, her refusal to do all the household chores without her husband's help, her serving a meal not pleasing to him, or a similar incident. What follows is inevitable. She may become the object of any or all of the following assaults: punching with fists, choking, kicking, knifing, slamming against a wall, throwing to the floor, or shoving down the stairs. Sometimes even threats with a gun have been reported. When the beating is over, the couple move into the third phase. The batterer feels guilty about what he has done. He is sorry and may become loving towards her. He assures his wife that he will never do anything violent or hurtful to her again. At that moment, he may believe he will never hurt her again. She wants to believe him, hoping that he will change. However, even with professional help, the tension building and the beatings may continue.

Why Do Women Stay?

Women have learned that it may be their own feelings of fear, guilt, or shame that keep them in a relationship that is physically abusive. Often, social and economic pressures compel a woman to stay. Sometimes she stays for lack of somewhere to go for shelter and advice or because she still feels that she loves her husband and that he might change, if only she can "hang in there." Tragically, in most cases, the abuse continues, for in fact her husband's behavior has nothing to do with her actions.

Other reasons for staying with him may seem as compelling. A woman may feel that a divorce is wrong and that she should keep her marriage together at all costs. Perhaps she feels her children need a father. She may be isolated with no outside job and few friends. The friends and relatives she does talk to may give her little support, perhaps because her situation frightens them and they don't want to admit to themselves that such violence could occur. If she confides in a counselor, she may also be encouraged to "save the marriage." And, along with her emotional dependence, she may worry about being able to find a job to support herself and her children. If she has her husband arrested, he may not be able to support her. If she doesn't have him arrested, he may beat her even more severely for trying to leave him. Is there a way out? Most women suffer these attacks for years before they finally find the courage and determination to take steps to keep from being victims of further abuse.

What Can a Battered Woman Do?

The first step for a woman to take is to *admit to herself that she is being abused* and that she is not being treated fairly. She has the right to feel safe from physical harm, especially in her own home.

Emergency Action

A woman can do a number of things to protect herself. She can hide extra money, car keys, and important documents somewhere safe so that she can get to them in a hurry. The phone number of the police department should be handy. She should have a place to go, such as an emergency shelter, a social service agency, or the home of a trusted friend or relative.

During an actual attack, the woman should defend herself as best she can. As soon as she is able, she should call the police and get their names and badge numbers in case she needs a record of the attack. Most importantly, she should leave the house and take her children with her. She may need medical attention, too, because she might be hurt more severely than she realizes. Having a record of her injuries, including photographs, can protect her legally should she decide to press charges.

Long-Range Plans

A woman needs to talk to people who can help. Good friends can lend support and guidance. Organizations that are devoted to women's concerns and not bound by society's traditions can assist her. They might help her explore her options in new ways. Emergency shelters for women, hotlines, women's organizations, social service agencies, community mental health centers, and hospital emergency rooms are all possible sources of support.

The following organizations have information about state contacts and shelters where a battered woman can go for help:

- Center for Women Policy Studies
  2000 P Street, N.W., #508
  Washington, DC 20036
  (202) 872-1770

- National Coalition Against Domestic
  Violence
  1728 N Street, N.W.
  Washington, DC 20036

Above all, a woman has to determine her own best course of action. Positive measures such as confiding in a relative, talking seriously with a friend, or consulting with a counselor are steps in the right direction. With the help of informal and formal help sources, including individual counseling for the husband as well as herself, a woman may be able to bring an end to the problem.

It has been observed that abused women need to develop better feelings about themselves—that is, change their self-image. In a book, "Stopping Wife Abuse," by Jennifer Baker Fleming, the following attitudes are suggested as positive and useful:

- I am not to blame for being beaten and abused.
- I am not the cause of another's violent behavior.
- I do not like it or want it.
- I do not have to take it.
- I am an important human being.
- I am a worthwhile woman.
- I deserve to be treated with respect.
- I do have power over my own life.
- I can use my power to take good care of myself.
- I can decide for myself what is best for me.
- I can make changes in my life if I want to.
- I am not alone. I can ask others to help me.
- I am worth working for and changing for.
- I deserve to make my own life safe and happy.

Prevention

Since there is no one cause of wife abuse, there is no easy way to prevent it. Until society rejects its tolerance and acceptance of violence for resolving conflict and expressing anger, meaningful changes in family relationships will not occur. Prevention starts with people changing their attitudes toward violence and women. No one deserves to be beaten or physically threatened, no matter what the excuse. It is a crime to beat anyone—a stranger, a friend, or your wife—and the law should be enforced. The tolerance of family violence as a way of life in one generation encourages family violence in another generation. Since the wife abuser didn't learn to deal with anger appropriately as a child, he handles his frustrations through aggression. He needs to know that it's human to feel anger, but inhuman to release those feelings by beating others. By learning to deal with these emotions through acceptable behavior, he can gain respect for himself and others. It's another positive step towards developing mutual respect in the husband/wife relationship where each sees the other as a worthy human being.

ANSWER SHEET

TEST NO. ________________ PART ______ TITLE OF POSITION ____
(AS GIVEN IN EXAMINATION ANNOUNCEMENT - INCLUDE OPTION, IF ANY)

PLACE OF EXAMINATION ____ DATE ____________
(CITY OR TOWN) (STATE)

RATING

USE THE SPECIAL PENCIL. MAKE GLOSSY BLACK MARKS.

1 A B C D E	26 A B C D E	51 A B C D E	76 A B C D E	101 A B C D E
2 A B C D E	27 A B C D E	52 A B C D E	77 A B C D E	102 A B C D E
3 A B C D E	28 A B C D E	53 A B C D E	78 A B C D E	103 A B C D E
4 A B C D E	29 A B C D E	54 A B C D E	79 A B C D E	104 A B C D E
5 A B C D E	30 A B C D E	55 A B C D E	80 A B C D E	105 A B C D E
6 A B C D E	31 A B C D E	56 A B C D E	81 A B C D E	106 A B C D E
7 A B C D E	32 A B C D E	57 A B C D E	82 A B C D E	107 A B C D E
8 A B C D E	33 A B C D E	58 A B C D E	83 A B C D E	108 A B C D E
9 A B C D E	34 A B C D E	59 A B C D E	84 A B C D E	109 A B C D E
10 A B C D E	35 A B C D E	60 A B C D E	85 A B C D E	110 A B C D E

Make only ONE mark for each answer. Additional and stray marks may be counted as mistakes. In making corrections, erase errors COMPLETELY.

11 A B C D E	36 A B C D E	61 A B C D E	86 A B C D E	111 A B C D E
12 A B C D E	37 A B C D E	62 A B C D E	87 A B C D E	112 A B C D E
13 A B C D E	38 A B C D E	63 A B C D E	88 A B C D E	113 A B C D E
14 A B C D E	39 A B C D E	64 A B C D E	89 A B C D E	114 A B C D E
15 A B C D E	40 A B C D E	65 A B C D E	90 A B C D E	115 A B C D E
16 A B C D E	41 A B C D E	66 A B C D E	91 A B C D E	116 A B C D E
17 A B C D E	42 A B C D E	67 A B C D E	92 A B C D E	117 A B C D E
18 A B C D E	43 A B C D E	68 A B C D E	93 A B C D E	118 A B C D E
19 A B C D E	44 A B C D E	69 A B C D E	94 A B C D E	119 A B C D E
20 A B C D E	45 A B C D E	70 A B C D E	95 A B C D E	120 A B C D E
21 A B C D E	46 A B C D E	71 A B C D E	96 A B C D E	121 A B C D E
22 A B C D E	47 A B C D E	72 A B C D E	97 A B C D E	122 A B C D E
23 A B C D E	48 A B C D E	73 A B C D E	98 A B C D E	123 A B C D E
24 A B C D E	49 A B C D E	74 A B C D E	99 A B C D E	124 A B C D E
25 A B C D E	50 A B C D E	75 A B C D E	100 A B C D E	125 A B C D E

ANSWER SHEET

TEST NO. _____ PART _____ TITLE OF POSITION _____

PLACE OF EXAMINATION _____ DATE_____

(CITY OR TOWN)   (STATE)

RATING

USE THE SPECIAL PENCIL.   MAKE GLOSSY BLACK MARKS.

	A B C D E		A B C D E		A B C D E		A B C D E		A B C D E
1		26		51		76		101	
2		27		52		77		102	
3		28		53		78		103	
4		29		54		79		104	
5		30		55		80		105	
6		31		56		81		106	
7		32		57		82		107	
8		33		58		83		108	
9		34		59		84		109	
10		35		60		85		110	

Make only ONE mark for each answer.   Additional and stray marks may be
counted as mistakes.   In making corrections, erase errors COMPLETELY.

	A B C D E		A B C D E		A B C D E		A B C D E		A B C D E
11		36		61		86		111	
12		37		62		87		112	
13		38		63		88		113	
14		39		64		89		114	
15		40		65		90		115	
16		41		66		91		116	
17		42		67		92		117	
18		43		68		93		118	
19		44		69		94		119	
20		45		70		95		120	
21		46		71		96		121	
22		47		72		97		122	
23		48		73		98		123	
24		49		74		99		124	
25		50		75		100		125	